"The authors say their _____ .u snatter 'the myth of the undeserving poor', to share a big vision of both what the Bible says about poverty and what can practically be done. Not only do they succeed, but they also provide a pithy historical and theological overview of the duty placed on Christians to 'act justly and to love mercy'. Building on both Catholic Social Teaching and the Evangelical thinking of John Stott, Francis Schaeffer, Leslie Newbiggin, and others, they remind us that Scripture teaches that 'every single person is created in the image of God, known by him and loved by him' – and of the responsibilities which this entails. Their repudiation of the stigmatisation of the poor as benefits cheats, as a feckless underclass of chavs and scroungers, is as welcome as their practical suggestions about how we can turn Food Bank Britain into a fairer and less socially divided society."

Lord David Alton, Crossbench Peer and Professor of Citizenship at Liverpool John Moores University

"As a local church leader, I have found this book provoking, challenging and helpful. It sheds light on today's culture and attitudes, and in response lays a good biblical foundation for both the church leader and the individual Christian to follow."

Paul Mann, senior leader, King's Church Hastings

"Over a century ago, William Booth and the Salvation Army shattered the Victorian myth of the undeserving poor. Martin Charlesworth and Natalie Williams issue *a similar challenge to a new generation. Is your reaction to poverty shaped unthinkingly by the media and by politicians? Don't let them do the thinking for you. Everyone should read this excellent and challenging book."*

Phil Moore, senior leader of Everyday Church, London, and author of *Gagging Jesus* and the *Straight to the Heart* series of devotional commentaries

"This book sets out the Church's responsibility to walk with, as well as to serve, the poor among us. Along the way it powerfully challenges stereotypes, and encourages a deeper, constructive and longer lasting engagement with the issues that cause and sustain poverty, as well as the way our attitude and actions need to change. This is an important and helpfully provocative book."

Dr Dave Landrum, Director of Advocacy, Evangelical Alliance

"Challenging, prophetic, incredibly timely, this book is essential reading for anyone who's concerned about the recent growth in inequality and poverty in our society. God has a lot to say in the Bible about poor people and how He expects them to be treated. We've drifted a long way from these truths. We're in danger of buying in to the myths, perhaps because they are more comfortable. This is a welcome call to get our policy and our practice back on track."

Chris Mould, Chairman, The Trussell Trust foodbank network

THE MYTH OF THE UNDESERVING POOR

A CHRISTIAN RESPONSE TO POVERTY IN BRITAIN TODAY

MARTIN CHARLESWORTH
&
NATALIE WILLIAMS

Grosvenor House
Publishing Limited

First published 2014 by Jubilee+ Ltd
www.jubilee-plus.org

ISBN 978-1-78148-875-1
e-ISBN: 978-1-78148-320-6

Cover design by Mark Titheridge, Visual Advance.
Typeset, printed and bound by Grosvenor House Publishing Limited.

CONTENTS

Acknowledgements

There are many people who have played a part in this book being written and published. Firstly, special thanks is due to the Jubilee+ team, for your prayers and support, and particularly to Sue Lyndon for proof-reading, Pete Lyndon for encouragement, and Geoff Knott for too many things to mention by name!

Thank you to Emma Farren and Annmarie Moran for your tireless research on our behalf. Thank you to Phil Moore, Chris Mould, Emma Farren, Geoff Knott and Paul Mann for valuable feedback on the draft text.

We have really appreciated the prayers, input and support of Nigel Ring, Dave Fellingham, Ginny Burgin, Andy & Ann McWilliam, Miles Jarvis, Graham Anns, Angela & Greg Kemm, Andy & Isla Biggs, Sheena Gardner and Andrew Westerman – thank you.

Jeremy Simpkins and David Stroud have each played a key part in the Jubilee+ journey – thank you for your oversight and passion for what we are doing.

Thank you to Paul Mann and King's Church Hastings for releasing Natalie to serve on the Jubilee+ team.

Martin would also like to thank his wife Jane, his family and the leaders and members of Barnabas Community Church in Shrewsbury for the many ways they have supported him in this project.

Natalie would also like to thank Dorothy Bourdet, Santino & Emma Hamberis, Hannah Beaney, Richard & Anna Wilson, Jo Thurston, and Andrew Wilson (along with many other friends who also prayed or discussed and debated this subject with her), and her mum.

Jubilee +

ABOUT JUBILEE+

Jubilee+ equips churches of all denominations to engage more effectively with our communities and particularly to help churches increase their capacity to serve the poor. We do this through a wide range of projects and initiatives, such as training leaders, providing resources, bringing encouragement, establishing networks, conducting research, developing relationships with partner organisations, and running conferences.

We hope we will be an encouragement as we, together, seek to enable the Church to be highly effective in its integrated mission to preach Christ and demonstrate his love for our communities.

Find us at: jubilee-plus.org | facebook.com/jubileeplus | twitter.com/jubileeplus

About the Authors

Martin Charlesworth

Martin lives in Shrewsbury with his wife Jane and has three grown-up daughters. He holds degrees in history and theology, and worked as a teacher and in business before becoming a church leader. Martin led Barnabas Community Church Shrewsbury from 1994 to 2014 and helped develop its strong emphasis on social action and community engagement.

In his spare time, Martin enjoys cycling, squash and mountaineering. He is an enthusiastic traveller, having previously lived in Pakistan and South Africa.

Martin leads Jubilee+.

Natalie Williams

Natalie grew up in a working class family in Hastings, one of the most deprived areas of Britain. She was the first person in her family to go to university. After graduating, she worked as a journalist in London and Beijing. She has an MA in Political Communications, with a particular emphasis on media narratives.

Natalie now works for King's Church Hastings and the New Ground family of churches. She is passionate about Christians and churches being a force for good in their communities.

Natalie is the Jubilee+ Communications Coordinator.

FOREWORD

William Booth wrote a seminal book that transformed nineteenth-century attitudes towards the poor. The founder of the Salvation Army demolished the Victorian myth that financial hardship was a largely self-inflicted punishment which rightly fell upon the undeserving poor. He asked his nation:

"When, in the streets of London, a cab horse trips and falls and lies stretched out in the midst of the traffic, there is no question of debating how he came to stumble before we get him on his legs again... if not for its own sake, then merely in order to prevent an obstruction to the traffic."

In the same way, he argued, any healthy society must help its poorest members first and ask questions of them later. William Booth's book inspired a more compassionate view towards the poor. It was a major contributor to the founding of the welfare state in Britain in the years which followed.

Martin Charlesworth and Natalie Williams have written a similar book for our own times. The modern welfare state is several decades old, and it shows. All of the main political parties agree that some reform is needed. But somewhere, in the midst of the debating and deliberating, has emerged a fresh hostility and anger towards a sector of society who are dubbed the undeserving poor. We are standing at a crossroads in our attitudes and I am so glad that we have this excellent book to challenge and to guide us.

Jesus talked a lot about people's attitudes towards the poor. He said that how we treat the least of his brothers and sisters is a greater indicator of our love towards him than the correctness of our doctrine and the volume of our singing. He warned us in Matthew 25:45: *"Truly I tell you, whatever you did not do for one of the least of these, you did not do for me."*

That's why you need to read this book, and you need to read it slowly on your knees. The authors approach this subject with a mountain of wisdom and a depth of sensitivity. They issue a clear warning and provocation to our generation. My prayer is that you will listen as closely to them as the Victorians listened to the wisdom of William Booth.

Phil Moore
Senior leader of Everyday Church, London, and author
of *Gagging Jesus* and the *Straight to the Heart* series of
devotional commentaries

Section 1

INTRODUCTION

Jesus came to bring good news to the poor. He wasn't ashamed to associate with people who were in desperate need; in fact, those on the margins of society – shunned beggars, 'unclean' lepers, shamed prostitutes and despised tax collectors – seemed to be attracted by him and comfortable around him. Jesus valued everyone he met, regardless of their status, wealth, health or faith. He saw beyond reputations and stigma, recognising in every human life the image of God. Jesus called (and still calls) his disciples to do likewise, but how much are Christians shaped by political narratives rather than God's narrative over a person? Is our behaviour towards particular groups of people influenced more by our culture or by our God? Are our attitudes shaped by the headlines we read in our newspapers or the verses we read in the Bible?

In 21st century Britain this is an enormous challenge for the Church. Research conducted in 2011 by the Organisation for Economic Co-operation and Development (OECD) revealed that inequality between the richest and poorest has risen faster in Britain than in any other developed country since 1975. This is despite the fact that public services "have more of a levelling effect on inequality in Britain than almost anywhere else".[1] Paradoxically, though concern about British poverty is increasing – in July 2014, research institute Ipsos-MORI recorded a level of concern among the British public about poverty/inequality that was higher than ever before[2] – attitudes towards those in poverty are hardening. Support for welfare spending "is at a historical low and appears to be moving in line with political policy and rhetoric rather than economic circumstance".[3] As poverty in Britain spreads and deepens,[4] negative perceptions about those in poverty spread and deepen too, with the public increasingly likely to blame individual behaviour rather than societal explanations.[5]

The subjects of poverty and benefits are, in Britain, inextricably linked. So while concern about poverty rises, debate about poverty rages. It is almost a daily occurrence for articles about benefits or welfare to appear in British national newspapers and our TV networks are increasingly preoccupied with the subject of benefits and poverty too, commissioning and broadcasting programmes such as *Benefits Street* and *Breadline Kids* (Channel 4, 2014), *The Big Benefits Row* and *On Benefits & Proud* (Channel 5, 2014 and 2013 respectively), *Poor Kids* (BBC Four, 2011) and *Famous, Rich and Hungry* (BBC One, 2014). Politicians working to reform welfare and charities working to relieve poverty are publicly engaged in intense debate.[6] Leading figures in our churches are feeling compelled to speak up on what they have called "a national crisis".[7]

As the public discussion increasingly asks whether or not people in need really deserve help, is that the correct question for Christians to be asking? Is there such a thing as a correct Christian response? We aim to address these questions in this book, first by gaining an understanding of where we are and how we got here, which we explore through the chapters on the historical context, media narratives and our survey research. Then we explore what the Bible has to say about poverty, which is, of course, vitally important in forming a Christian perspective on how the poor should be treated. It also guides us in how to answer a crucial question: in a First World context, who are the poor?

Finally, we move on to the all-important question of how Christians should respond. Our answers to the previous questions impact upon how we think and how we act. There is a unique call placed on God's people to "act justly and to love mercy" (Micah 6:8) that Jesus leaves us no option but to take seriously. The gospel compels us to align our attitudes to God's heart concerning those who need justice and mercy. Then we need to act accordingly, expressing his kindness to those who are poor in our communities. Our beliefs, attitudes and behaviour need to be shaped by Jesus. It is time to expose the myth of the undeserving poor.

POVERTY IN BRITAIN

2.1

A complex
heritage of care
for the poor

'Come,' said Mr. Bumble, somewhat less pomp-
ously, for it was gratifying to his feelings to observe
the effect his eloquence had produced; 'Come,
Oliver! Wipe your eyes with the cuffs of your
jacket, and don't cry into your gruel; that's a very
foolish action, Oliver.' It certainly was, for there
was quite enough water in it already.

Charles Dickens's classic novel *Oliver Twist* (1838) has been immortalised through film and stage production. The story is well known. What is less well known is that the novel was written as a negative social commentary on the treatment of the poor through the Victorian work-house system in Britain. The central character, Oliver Twist, is an orphan who ends up under the care of the pompous and condescending workhouse keeper, Mr Bumble, whose social attitudes are expressed in profound disrespect for the poor and contempt for the reasons that have caused them to end up in the workhouses.

Through his novel, Dickens was entering into the long-standing debate about the treatment of the poor in British society. This debate stretched back across the centuries and involved questions about the role of State and Church – as well as questions about the true status of those who were the poor of the time. In this chapter we will take a look at some key aspects of this important story.

Throughout the long history of Christianity in Britain, the Church in its many forms has been instrumental in care for the poor. Every tradition of the Church has a significant social justice element in its heritage. The early Celtic Church espoused simplicity of lifestyle and direct charity. Then, during the Middle Ages, the Roman Catholic Church developed the monastic tradition in which educational, medical and social support for the needy was central. At that time, most practical care for the poor was done largely by the Church and it was considered a religious duty for all Christians to undertake the 'Seven Corporal Works of Mercy' based on the teachings of Jesus in Matthew 25.

The Reformation in the early sixteenth century brought about a number of significant changes concerning care for the poor. The new national churches replaced the Catholic Church as the State churches in Britain. At the same time the monasteries were abolished by Henry VIII, thus ending centuries of care for the poor through the work of monastic communities. The theology of the Church reformers suggested that the State had a responsibility for the poor and should create the structure for that care to happen effectively.

The key development of this period was the passing of the Poor Law legislation in 1601. This was one of the last Acts of Queen Elizabeth I's reign and was intended to provide the basis for a national system of care for the poor. The Poor Law empowered local magistrates to administer care for the poor based on the parish system of the Church of England. The parish authorities were directed to raise a local tax from parishes and home-owners and distribute it to the poor through appointed overseers and local parish churchwardens. Almshouses, hospitals, orphanages and workhouses were set up and employers were instructed to take the unemployed into their service wherever possible. The Elizabethan Poor Law – later known as 'The Old Poor Law' – became the basis for provision for the poor in Britain for several centuries, although it was modified on various occasions during the eighteenth and nineteenth centuries.

There are two aspects of the Poor Law that are especially significant and relevant to our discussion – the emerging partnership between Church and State, and the strong differentiation of categories among the poor. We need to pause and reflect on each of these points because they are both fundamental to our discussion.

The Poor Law was not centrally administered – it was locally enacted and each locality was defined in terms of the Church's parish structure. This was not only about geography; it was about manpower and local knowledge. The churchwardens became key players in the administration of relief and the church itself was responsible for providing local knowledge of the economic status of residents in each parish. To put it simply, poor relief could not have been done without the Church. So the Poor Law laid the foundation of a clear partnership between State and Church in caring for the poor. This partnership endured to varying degrees for several centuries.

The Elizabethan Poor Law also brought about a formal distinction between and categorisation of the poor. Four groups were identified: children; the aged and infirm; the genuinely unemployed; and the so-called wilfully idle. Those too young, old or sick to work were to be cared for; those who could work were to be found opportunities or given relief; and the apparently work-shy were to be given harsh corrective treatment to persuade them to change their minds. Such treatments theoretically included corporal punishment, jail, forced labour or even banishment – although enforcement of these sanctions was very inconsistent. However, the distinction between the 'deserving' and 'undeserving' poor was now established in British culture and society and enshrined in law.

As Britain moved from being an agricultural to a largely industrial society, it became necessary to reform the Poor Law fundamentally to address the specific and growing issue of urban poverty. The Poor Law Amendment Act of 1834 – 'the New Poor Law' – established a more uniform system based on the development of a nationwide network of workhouses. Workhouses were to be based on groups of parishes and poor relief was to be only available at the workhouses.

Conditions in the workhouses were intended to be such that they were not an attractive option for any who could find work elsewhere. The outcomes of the New Poor Law were usually harsh, as pointed out by nineteenth century social critics such as Charles Dickens, as we noted above. In fact, the New Poor Law represented a hardening of social attitudes towards poverty. Considerable social stigma was attached to the workhouses and popular culture increasingly saw the poor as blameworthy in their plight. The New Poor Law also saw a decline in the role of churches in the relief of poverty. Many church leaders expressed opposition to the harsh terms of the legislation and local churches were no longer significantly involved in the implementation of it. However, churches did continue to provide chaplaincy and other support to workhouse inmates.

This New Poor Law, along with various other Victorian public health and local government policies, formed the basis of British social policy until the turn of the twentieth century. With the coming of the new century the foundations for the modern welfare state were gradually being established. The focus moved from providing poor relief to finding ways of eliminating poverty. Structural economic issues came into focus and the State widened the scope of its commitment to tackling poverty. It began to provide some universal benefits during the pre-First World War period with the establishment of state pensions (1908) and sickness and unemployment insurance (1911).

The Poor Law system was finally abolished in 1948 with the advent of the modern welfare state, which we look at in more detail in the next chapter. The foundational ethos of the welfare state was to treat all citizens as equals and to use an insurance system as a basis for providing universal access to social provisions such as education, health care, pensions, sickness and unemployment benefits. Of critical importance to this ethos was the refusal (at least in principle) to categorise the poor – no longer were they to be deserving or undeserving. Central to our discussion will be the issue of whether more recent political and social developments have brought back distinctions and categorisations among the poor and needy within British society. We will explore this in a later chapter.

Meanwhile, we need to reflect further on the role of the Church as the State increased its capacity and took the central role in shaping and enacting policy towards poor relief. Overall, the Church has had a difficult relationship with the various phases of Poor Law provision in Britain. While being involved in the process, there has been consistent unease about the injustices frequently associated with the legislation. There have been many critics within the Church of both the philosophy and the methodology of the Poor Law. In contrast, the early development of the ideology and implementation of the twentieth century welfare state met with much more support from church leaders.

However, since the Reformation, the principal social energy of the Church in Britain has been channelled into its own initiatives to help the poor rather than into those established by the State. Numerous examples could be given from every century. But there is one overarching factor that warrants our specific attention – the astonishing social energy arising from the eighteenth century Methodist movement, which gathered further pace in the nineteenth century. John Wesley's concern for, and emphasis on, the relief of poverty and injustice was central to his theology and practice: he gave every encouragement to Methodists to address social problems directly. He had a special interest in such widely different issues as extending educational provision, abolishing slavery, improving working conditions, improving health, reducing alcoholism, and factory reform. By the end of the eighteenth century, Methodism had become the social conscience of the British Church.

During the nineteenth century, the influence of Methodism spread into both the Anglican Church and the other free churches. This led, in turn, to an astonishing development of Church philanthropy and political activism. Christians became the leaders of much of the social activism of the time, in such areas as prison reform, education, factory reform, the abolition of slavery, the development of sanitation, child labour reform and temperance. Well known leaders such as William Wilberforce, the 7th Earl of Shaftesbury and Elizabeth Fry were supported by many thousands of highly motivated Christians who believed that part of their mission in life was to improve the lot of their fellow citizens wherever they could do so.

Despite the huge influence of the Church in the nineteenth century, the first half of the twentieth century saw a significant decline in its size, energy and influence in Britain. Also, crucially, the Church lost much of its social vision. The reasons for this relative decline are complex and multi-faceted. They included the impact of two world wars, the influence of liberal theology, the slow rise of secularism and the apparent challenge to faith of modern science. Evangelicals, in particular, were on the retreat during this time. They tended to focus on a personal gospel and the battle to survive the cultural onslaught of both secularism and liberal theology. In fact, many evangelicals deliberately withdrew from social engagement due to associating what they then called 'the social gospel' with liberal Christianity! Some who focused on helping the poor had moved away from sharing the gospel, but the attempt to redress the balance swung the pendulum far in the opposite direction. The second half of the twentieth century was more hopeful, but we'll come to that in the next chapter.

2.2

The era of the welfare state

British attitudes towards the poor and helping the poor have oscillated over the last century or so: the prevalent Victorian mindset saw poverty as largely the result of individual idleness, while the impact of the Second World War and the accompanying austerity led to widespread support for the creation of a system of welfare that would care for everyone in need 'from the cradle to the grave'.

While the foundations for the modern welfare state were laid in the first half of the twentieth century (as we saw in the previous chapter), Christian leaders emerged at the forefront of developing solutions to poverty in 1940s wartime Britain. Then-Archbishop of Canterbury, William Temple, popularised the term 'welfare state' and Anglican, Catholic and other church leaders were among the leading voices calling for the abolition of extreme inequalities of wealth. Temple's seminal book *Christianity and Social Order* (1942) was hugely influential in the development of the welfare state – in it he called on the Government to address increasing poverty and deprivation in Britain. It was a friend and contemporary of Temple and RH Tawney (another leading Christian thinker of the time), William Beveridge, whose 1942 report established the blueprint for doing exactly that. The *Beveridge Report* is seen by some as "a practical outworking of [Temple's] theological position".[8] This is not at all to suggest that the Church was the architect of the welfare state, but rather that the influence of Christians and their social values on the senior politicians and civil servants of all persuasions at this time were highly significant.

The *Beveridge Report* set out a system of lifelong support designed to ensure no one in Britain would languish in poverty, but all would be guaranteed a certain minimum standard of living. It was based on Christian values of human dignity, equality, and concern for one's neighbour, with Archbishop Temple stating that it was "the first time anyone had set out to embody the whole spirit of the Christian ethic in an Act of Parliament".[9] Yet it placed the State at the very heart of tackling deprivation: the report saw the State as intrinsic to the creation of "a national minimum" but thought that it "should leave room and encouragement for voluntary action by each individual to provide more than that minimum for himself and his family".[10] The *Beveridge Report* attracted huge support from the public.

A series of Parliamentary Acts followed, introducing comprehensive benefits for every member of society, extending National Insurance, sick pay, annual leave, pensions, free education and income even for the unemployed, and introducing the National Health Service. Britain was radically changed, as were the lives of countless men, women and children who had been or would come to be in need. Christian principles had played a key role in these changes and, by not discriminating against anyone facing poverty, the new legislation made progress towards doing away with notions of a deserving and an undeserving poor.

The ambition was not to create a dependency culture – in fact, attempts to improve education and achieve zero unemployment ran alongside the creation of the welfare state, which was designed to slay the 'giant evils' of not just want, ignorance, squalor and disease, but also idleness. Neither was it a handout: the idea was that citizens would pay into the system so that, in their time of need, they could receive back the support they required. The grand vision was to give anyone in need a hand-up from the State – the minimum standard of living should form a springboard that each individual could use to further improve their lives. This is possibly why there was a general political agreement (spanning three decades) about the State's responsibility to care for the most vulnerable members of society. As British sociologist T. H. Marshall wrote in 1965, at that time there was still a general consensus that "the overall responsibility for the welfare of citizens must remain with the state".[11]

However, in the 1980s a confluence of factors caused this broad agreement to fracture. For example, the National Health Service had, in one sense, become a victim of its own success, helping people to live longer but therefore increasing the demand without the means to meet it. There was a growing claim from some quarters that State intervention was eroding a sense of personal responsibility. Indeed, through a series of small but significant changes, the welfare state had moved far from what Beveridge envisaged. The contribution-based system that would provide a safety net for those who fall on hard times and a springboard back into an improved quality of life started to be seen by many to be failing. In tandem, the perception that the benefits system provides a comfortable lifestyle choice for those who are unwilling to work started to gain traction.

Meanwhile the role of the Church in society had, on the whole, receded into the background: following peak attendance rates in the 1950s, churches hit a sudden crisis of decline in the 1960s. Attempts to stem the tide (as well as the cultural drift towards secularism) led to large sections of the Church shifting their focus towards individual salvation rather than the common good. Among Christians, some criticised others for focusing too much on caring for the poor, to the extent that social action became synonymous, for some, with a watered down gospel that met physical needs while almost ignoring the deeper spiritual need.

As Margaret Thatcher set about 'rolling back the State' (partly in response to a perceived sense of entitlement that had started to emerge), a renewed hardening of attitudes towards the poor developed – particularly towards the unemployed. Since 1985, British Social Attitudes surveys have shown a significant decline in public belief that the Government should provide a decent standard of living for the unemployed (81% in 1985, down to a low of 50% in 2006). Likewise, there is now very little support from the public for the Government to increase its spending on social security – while 13% prioritised this in 1990, only five per cent prioritised it in 2012 and, unusually, the recession did not lead to any shift in public support for it. Furthermore, the 2013 British Social Attitudes survey found that "support for additional spending on welfare benefits for the poor is considerably lower now than it was when the question was first asked in 1987... much of this decline occurred in the 1990s".[12] The survey discovered that the number of people who feel that the Government's first or second priority in terms of welfare spending should focus on the unemployed has fallen from 32% in 1983 to just 12% in 2012.

Just as the gap between the rich and the poor in the UK widens faster than in any other developed country – the wealthiest 10% in our society now earn 12 times as much as the poorest 10%[13] – so another troubling gap widens: public perceptions of welfare are increasingly distant from the reality. For example, under Margaret Thatcher's Government the proportion of Gross Domestic Product spent on welfare actually increased, only beginning to decline in 1993; then, in 2002 under Tony Blair's administration, the chunk of GDP spent on welfare actually reached a pre-1950 low. It began to rise again in 2008, in connection with the financial crisis, but when the Conservative-Liberal Democrat Coalition Government came to power in 2010, it introduced austerity measures to reduce it again.[14]

According to the British Government's definition of poverty – households living with an income below 60% of the median household income – and its own statistics released in 2014, almost a quarter of working-age adults in the UK are living in absolute poverty[15] and over 20 million people are in poverty as a whole.[16] The previous year was the first time that children living in poverty were twice as likely to come from a working household than from one in which no adult works. Responding to this, Child Poverty Action Group's Alison Garnham said: "Despite all the talk about 'scroungers' and generations of families never working, today's poverty figures expose comprehensively the myth that the main cause of poverty is people choosing not to work. The truth is that for a growing number of families work isn't working."[17]

These rises in poverty do not seem to be eroding an increasing harshness towards the poor in Britain today. Figures from the long-standing British Social Attitudes Survey have surprised researchers, who say: "The current, prolonged economic downturn has had little discernible impact [on attitudes towards welfare];

unemployment stands at its highest point in 15 years, yet this appears to have made no obvious dent on the view that unemployment benefits are too high. This is not at all the trend we would have expected based on experience of the previous recession."[18] The rhetoric of a deserving and undeserving poor has re-emerged with great force, with public debate on this issue played out in the media on an almost daily basis. There is a widespread perception that many who are receiving help from the State are spending tax-payers' money on luxuries such as cigarettes, plasma TVs and holidays, while those who are working hard are struggling to make ends meet. A dominant narrative of 'strivers' versus 'skivers' – in which the strivers are the deserving poor and the skivers are the undeserving poor – is increasingly ingrained in public consciousness. In some of our national newspapers, words such as 'scroungers', 'feckless' and 'lazy' are now commonly used of those accessing welfare support – or 'pocketing handouts', as some of the press put it.

It is in this context that the Church has re-engaged in tackling poverty in a very public and inescapable way. "Faith communities almost disappeared from public view during the 1990s,"[19] as one *Guardian* journalist wrote in 2010. Whether the Church retreated from public life or was relegated to the background by an increasingly secular society is a subject for much debate but, either way, the State's expanding responsibility for the poorest members of society ran in parallel with the Church becoming increasingly marginalised. Notably, renewal of the evangelical Church in recent years has gradually led to a redevelopment of its social vision. Church leaders and theologians have played a crucial role in reminding the Church of its biblical mandate to care for the poor and engage with society.

Social justice is central to the Church's agenda once more. Yet the context is very different now. The competence and scale of the State's role in welfare is in serious doubt. The ever-advancing State provision of the twentieth century now looks like a thing of the past. State cutbacks are ongoing and unlikely to be reversed for many years to come. The Church is being invited back to the table of social policy discussion in a significant way. The State now needs the Church once again to share the burden of welfare provision and care for the poor. The long eroded partnership of State and Church is being reinvented – to the surprise of many in the Church and to the consternation of avowed secularists. But the simple fact is that the Church has vital social energy, huge social capital and an army of volunteers who are willing to turn their hands to the task of caring for the poor in new and creative ways.

It is in this context that the question of the status and value of the poor becomes a burning issue for the Church once more. What do we think of the tendency in our current culture to reinstate the division between the deserving and undeserving poor? And how are our convictions on this issue going to influence the way we care for the poor and seek to shape our wider culture?

2.3

The Church: thinking, speaking, acting

There has been no shortage of Christian responses to the issues raised by poverty in recent years. Church leaders have hit the headlines time and again as they have commented on levels of poverty, benefits policies, unemployment, bankers' bonuses and a host of related subjects. And behind those church leaders are numerous activists, local church groups, writers, theologians, charities, entrepreneurs and researchers who are all engaging vigorously with poverty in the UK.

The financial crisis of 2007-2008 was undoubtedly a trigger for the remarkable rise in Church engagement and active commitment to the relief of poverty. This has been widely and positively noted in the media and among policy-makers. However, the Church's intensified engagement has also created a number of challenges. Firstly, the subsequent reform of the benefits system has become a key debating point between Government and sections of the Church. Secondly, the dramatic rise of church-based foodbanks has been both widely applauded and widely critiqued as a response to poverty. These are only two of many similar issues, but they happen to have hit the headlines time and again and have come to symbolise the ongoing challenge of how best to tackle poverty.

THEOLOGICAL ROOTS

Looking beyond these headlines, there are deep theological roots behind the current high level of engagement by the Church in tackling poverty.

The Catholic Church has a robust tradition in the principles of so-called CST – Catholic Social Teaching.[20] In recent years, Catholics have been re-energised by the stance on poverty taken by Pope Francis, who has frequently articulated that care for the poor is a priority.[21] Archbishop Vincent Nicholls and Catholic politician Lord Alton have been eminent spokesmen of Catholic social teaching in the UK context.[22]

Churches of a more liberal theological persuasion characteristically emphasise the Christian duty to "love your neighbour as yourself" (Matthew 22:39) alongside the prophetic responsibility of the Church to speak up for justice. It is no surprise that churches with these values have also been vociferous about and actively engaging with poverty in recent years. Many members of such churches are both supporters of social action initiatives and critics of the apparent widening of the divide between rich and poor.[23]

However, the most striking aspect of this issue is the vigorous response of evangelical churches in both theological reflection and practical activism. This would have been hard to predict 50 years ago when evangelicalism in Britain was much less dynamic than it is now. In those days, the focus was mainly on theological defence against the apparent advances of liberal theology and secular society. The gospel was interpreted personally but not socially. Politics was secular. Social action was secondary. Popular pietism prevailed. It was arguably John Stott's contribution that most changed the mindset of evangelical churches in the late twentieth century. Specifically, his book *Issues Facing Christians Today*,[24] first published in 1984, provided a robust biblical case for the social engagement of the Church. It proved to be a watershed. Stott and other thinkers such as Francis Schaeffer, Leslie Newbiggin, Alan Kreider, Jim Wallis, Tim Keller and Richard Foster helped to lay the theological foundations that are now shaping much evangelical church culture and social engagement. Stott's influence, in particular, has been widely acknowledged.

As we survey the scene today we can see a recent trend for church leaders to focus more on social engagement and social justice issues. In addition to Stott, there are a few other notable influencers who have been significant in shaping the culture of the Church and specifically its current response to poverty issues. They are all strong advocates of the Church's social engagement. Among them are Anglican leaders Rowan Williams, John Sentamu and Justin Welby. Others from diverse backgrounds include Pope Francis, Andy Hawthorne of the Message Trust, Steve Chalke of the Oasis Trust, and the late Simon Pettit of Newfrontiers. These leaders represent a wide variety of constituencies within the Christian world. Their teaching and example is shaping the outlook of tens of thousands of Christians in Britain and beyond.

THE EMERGING GRASSROOTS SOCIAL ACTION NETWORKS – THE BIG SURPRISE!

Interestingly, the most important response to current British poverty has not come from prominent church leaders or even from established charities, but from organisations started in recent years to tackle specific social needs through setting up local projects linked to church communities. There are literally dozens of newly started initiatives developing social action across all sectors of need. However, a decisive and exciting aspect of this is that some initiatives have been able to create a methodology of reproducing their work quickly and effectively across the nation. This process is known as 'community franchising', which uses some of the principles of business franchising – but for community benefit. These franchises originate with a vision to respond to a particular social need. Then they grow by creating a methodology, developing training, and then offering to partner with and equip local churches to provide their particular service in a given locality. Crucially, governance for the local projects is primarily within the local churches or with other local bodies – not with the central organisation. Thus these community franchises equip and empower local churches to meet social needs in a strategic and cost-effective way. Some have grown dramatically and quickly become nationally known. Prominent examples include Street Pastors,[25] Christians Against Poverty,[26] Community Money Advice[27] and the Trussell Trust (foodbanks)[28]. But what most people don't know is that there are several dozen other franchises doing great work – and new ones being created all the time.[29]

The current community franchise movement started in the 1990s but has grown dramatically since the financial crisis of 2007-2008. This was a powerful catalyst. The movement has also been helped by a generally favourable response from Government. Alongside this, national networks of Christian community franchisors have been formed and their leaders are able to collaborate and learn from one another relatively easily.[30]

The scope and impact of community franchises is dramatic. They have mobilised thousands of committed volunteers, spread their influence over the country and been a vehicle for a grassroots response to social need and poverty. Our own Jubilee+ research has found that, within churches, literally millions of hours are given to volunteering in projects that serve the poor.[31] Politicians have woken up to find that the Church is far more dynamic and engaged than they had expected or even believed to be possible.

CHRISTIAN ATTITUDES TO THE POOR

Our society faces a challenging mix of issues: austerity, personal indebtedness, benefits cuts, housing shortages, service cutbacks, significant unemployment and increasing economic inequality. There are no easy answers. The multiple issues before the nation have provoked deep heart-searching and difficult questions. Whose fault is it that we are facing these issues? Is it governments past and present? Is it the state of the world economy? Is it the bankers? Or are the poor sometimes to blame themselves? Are they just avoiding work, lounging on the sofa all day watching TV and cheating on benefits claims? As we noted in the previous chapter, there has been a resurgence of the old distinction between the deserving and undeserving poor and 'hoodies', 'chavs', 'the feckless underclass' and 'benefit scroungers' are assuming a significant place in our media narratives on poverty.

How has the Church responded to this talk of the undeserving poor? In the public arena, Church leaders and activists are very reluctant to make the type of value judgements underlying the label 'undeserving poor'. The Church Urban Fund has articulated a significant approach to poverty, arguing that it is complex and multi-dimensional and cannot be reduced to simple definitions. Its own definition includes the three dimensions of resources, relationships and identity. It advocates a long-term, strategic and relational approach to the relief of poverty based on the intrinsic dignity of every person. There is no room in their analysis for making simplistic moralistic distinctions between categories of the poor. This approach is widely echoed across the range of Christian community franchise charities, which affirm the universal accessibility of their services.

One of the strongest rebuttals to media talk of the undeserving poor has come from the Joint Public Issues team of the United Reformed Church, Church of Scotland, Methodist and Baptist Churches in a report entitled *The Lies We Tell Ourselves: Ending Comfortable Myths About Poverty*.[32] The report argues against the popular idea that the poor don't want to work, are mostly on drink and drugs, don't manage their money properly, are on the fiddle, and have an easy life on inflated benefits. It is hard-hitting stuff, backed up by specific research. Others have said similar things in less forceful ways, but this is one of the most coherent and forceful attempts by the churches to stand against popular media narratives.

Prominent church leaders have also stepped into this specific debate from time-to-time. For example, in 2012 then-Archbishop of Canterbury Rowan Williams warned against "a quiet resurgence of the seductive language of deserving and undeserving poor".[33] Meanwhile, Archbishop John Sentamu took a similar approach when speaking in the House of Lords. He dismissed the concept of the undeserving poor, saying that so-called scroungers were a "convenient scapegoat when it seems expedient to make sure someone pays the price of the hardship we fear... the Church has always been in the forefront of the challenge to speak and act prophetically, to give a voice to the voiceless and hope and help to those in need".[34]

2.4

Marginalised by the media: 'us and them'

Poverty in Britain has come under the media spotlight in a number of ways over the last few years, with a particularly renewed focus since the global recession of 2007-2008. From television documentaries about foodbanks, immigration, benefits claimants, and child poverty, to fierce debate in our national newspapers about whether those in need are deserving or undeserving of the support they receive, particularly from the State – the coverage has become ubiquitous.

The press are often accused of painting one-sided pictures, so we wanted to get to the heart of this and see if there really is a media narrative around poverty in Britain today. We sometimes think of the media as noisy background to our lives, but in fact they decide which issues make it into the public domain and how they are presented. It would be incredibly naive of us to believe that the media are just impartial bystanders merely observing what is happening and informing the public. Instead, they not only control what makes it onto the agenda, but they also frame the way in which issues are presented. Of course, they don't all frame the issues in the same way. But we would be equally naive to assume that the media we consume have no influence on us – for the vast majority of the public they are our main source of information about current affairs. We depend on them for knowledge about what is happening in the world around us. Both logically and biblically speaking, a steady diet of a particular way of thinking will begin to shape our views, whether that is simply by more deeply entrenching our preconceived ideas, or actually, over time, changing our views.

This media attention on poverty as an important issue in Britain coincides with an increase in 'conflictual framing', which perpetuates an 'us and them' agenda. In one sense, 'us and them' journalism is nothing new, even in regard to the poor. We've seen earlier in this section that discourse about the worthiness of the poor to receive help has been around for centuries. But this doesn't negate the damage such media narratives can do in shaping attitudes and perspectives by inducing fear and resentment of those who 'are not like us'. This is known as 'othering'.

One of the dominant ways by which 'othering' occurs is by raising the voices of 'us' while silencing the voices of 'them'. What this means in practice is not only that there is a very small number of reporters from the 'them' group (in this case, those in poverty), but also that the voices of those in poverty are often either entirely omitted from the news or only given a small space for their 'right of reply'. This contributes to lazy stereotyping, because many of those reporting on poverty in Britain are themselves far removed from it and from people in need. Where there is a vacuum of proximate experience, the door is wide open for media narratives to take root. It means we get an off-kilter news diet filtered through a very specific and narrow lens – one that is external looking in, rather than displaying any genuine experience of or affinity with those in poverty.

This isn't something specific to the poor – many different groups of people in Britain feel marginalised by the media too: Muslims, for example, and Christians too. In a survey I (Natalie) conducted in 2013 into how Christians feel about the British press, only seven of 409 respondents believe there is any British newspaper that portrays Christians 'very accurately', 42 per cent said there is not a single British newspaper that is 'pro-Christian', and only

23 participants feel represented in media coverage of Christians always or most of the time.[35]

However disappointed or disgruntled Christians and others may feel about the media coverage they receive, the marginalisation and 'othering' of people in poverty is distinctly more troubling. Firstly, because the poor are much less likely to mobilise in protest or action against the coverage they receive (or to have the means to do so), and secondly, because it strikes at the heart of a commitment to the common good and a shared sense of community that is vitally important if those in poverty are to raise themselves or to be raised out of their situations.

In order to take a snapshot of media coverage of poverty in Britain today, we selected 10 sources of news – BBC online, the Daily Mail, the Daily Mirror, The Guardian, the Huffington Post, The Independent, ITV online, The Sun, The Telegraph, and The Times – and analysed articles about poverty in Britain that appeared during a four-week period. The timeframe we selected – starting on 7 January 2014 – was directly after the first episode of controversial documentary Benefits Street aired on Channel 4, when we knew there was a high volume of coverage from both critics and defenders of the people represented by those featured in the programme. It also meant that we would be able to explore how different media outlets covered the same stories and events.

This resulted in 390 articles, of which 253 were news reports, 34 features, 95 comment pieces, five letters and three cartoons. All 390 articles were coded according to a framework that asked:

- *What is the main type of poverty mentioned?*
- *What other types of poverty are mentioned?*

- *Is there a positive, negative or neutral attitude towards the poor?*
- *How much space is given for the voices of the poor?*
- *Is the language used by the writer (i.e. not quoted speech) positive, negative or neutral towards the poor?*
- *What negative language is used to describe the poor?*
- *Are the poor portrayed as undeserving of help and/ or to blame for their situation?*

Whenever analysing media content, there is potential for subjectivity to sway the results. We attempted to counter this in two specific ways. Firstly, we asked an independent researcher to code all of the articles. Secondly, a selection of articles was coded by 10 different people as part of an 'inter-coder reliability' test – divergence in the results highlighted the areas that were particularly open to interpretation and enabled us to alter the code where necessary to reduce subjectivity, which we did.

Some of the results were unsurprising. For example, just over half of the articles (52%) focused on benefits claimants as the main type of poverty mentioned, which is to be expected due to the timing of the study. However, immigration, unemployment and criminal activity were also the focus for significant numbers of articles. The picture became more interesting when we explored secondary types of poverty that were introduced into articles that focused predominantly on another type of poverty. Here we saw criminal activity mentioned in 25% of articles (of which nine per cent was benefit fraud, whether alleged or actual). Well over a third of the mentions of criminal activity were in just one of the 10 media outlets: 37% came from the *Daily Mail*.

The findings become slightly more complex when we start to look at negativity towards the poor. In total, there were 78 articles that featured either a negative attitude towards the poor, negative language about the poor, or portrayed the poor as undeserving of help or to blame for their own situation. So, exactly a fifth of all of the articles about poverty in Britain during our four-week period were negative in one way or another towards those in need. Perhaps that sounds like a low number compared to what we might expect, but half of these came from news articles, which are supposed to be neutral, and that amounts to double the number of news articles featuring any positivity towards the poor.

Furthermore, when we drill down into the details we find that the negativity is weighted in certain places: three of our 10 media outlets featured no negativity whatsoever – *The Independent*, *The Telegraph* and *ITV* online – while others were disproportionately negative: the *Daily Mail* and *The Sun* accounted for 64% of all of the negative articles, with 41% and 36% (respectively) of their articles being negative towards the poor. A factor that makes this worse is that almost two-thirds of the negative *Daily Mail* articles were news items (63%), rather than comment pieces, where opinion and subjectivity are to be expected. (For *The Sun*, 33% came from the newspaper's news section.)

As we would expect from the previous paragraph, 60% of negative language towards the poor was found in these same two publications: words such as 'scroungers', 'lazy', 'feckless', 'cheating' and 'irresponsible' were chosen by the writers themselves (i.e. not used in quotations from sources). Likewise, 67% of articles portraying the poor as undeserving of help or to blame for their situation appeared in *The Sun* and the *Daily Mail*.

In relation to 'othering' though, where the voices of 'them' are suppressed and ignored, hardly any of the national media outlets in this study gave 'ample' space to the voices of the poor themselves (in this case 'ample' is defined as a quarter of the article or more). In fact, only 17 articles (four per cent) gave this kind of space to the voices of the poor; interestingly, 10 of those articles appeared in the *Daily Mirror* and *The Sun* tabloid newspapers (five in each). However, what the code doesn't reveal but the articles themselves do is that sometimes the 'ample space' given to those in poverty is actually used to perpetuate media narratives. For example, an article that appeared in *The Sun* on 8 January 2014 that features numerous quotes from people in poverty ran under the headline 'Cops to probe the thieves and cheats of Benefit Street' and the quotes followed a similar pattern, such as this one: *"I've been arrested 200 times and I've got 80 convictions. I'll grow out of it at some point, I hope."*

Our snapshot of media analysis found that 78% of the articles featured no space at all for those in poverty to tell their story, put across their point of view, or even say one sentence about their situation or in their defence. Only five of the negative articles afforded 'ample' space for the voices of the poor to be heard. The media outlets least likely to give any space for the poor to speak are not those we might expect: rather than those that are more negative towards those in poverty, it is the *Huffington Post*, *ITV* online and *The Independent* – two of which showed no negativity towards the poor at all – that very, very rarely give any space in their articles for the voices of the poor. In fact, the newspaper that is most negative towards the poor – the *Daily Mail* – is the second most likely to give space for them to be heard.

Our independent researcher was surprised at what she found. After reading and coding 390 articles, looking beneath the statistics from the code, the impression she detected was of a "thinly veiled attitude... that poverty is a character defect". If our main national media sources present, at best, no space for those in need to speak up or, at worst, negativity towards the poorest members of British society, does this have any bearing on how Christians do or should respond to those in poverty? A 2012 in-depth academic study that argued British newspapers "can be placed on a pro/anti religious continuum"[36] found the *Daily Mail* to be on the 'pro-Christian' end of the spectrum, indicating that one of the most 'pro-Christian' newspapers in Britain is also the most 'anti-poor'. This principle applies in the opposite direction, too, with *The Guardian* appearing at the secular/ anti-Christian end of the spectrum but being the media outlet most positive towards the poor in our study.

The key findings of our media analysis are a cause for serious concern. Firstly, the lack of neutrality towards the poor in a significant number of news articles is worrying – particularly because when reporters veer away from the path of impartiality, they drift towards negatively more often than positivity. Secondly – and more troubling still – is the finding that the poor do not have a voice in mainstream media. The fact that those in poverty are unlikely to be afforded space for their voices even in media that is broadly sympathetic to their plight is disturbing. This turns the issue of poverty into an issue of justice, too – it is imperative that Christians speak up for the voiceless.

These two particular trends exacerbate 'othering' – they perpetuate an 'us and them' mentality in which we cease to identify with those in need, instead seeing them as 'not like us'. One journalist describes this phenomenon as a "gradual erosion of empathy" where poor people "are an entirely different species" and "instead of being disgusted by poverty, we are disgusted by poor people themselves".[37] In a society where 70% of us don't even know the names of any of our neighbours,[38] let alone speak to them, we are increasingly reliant on the media to inform us about people we don't know. Therefore, if the media present us with an imbalanced view – or don't give us access to the voices of the most vulnerable and marginalised in society – there is a real danger that our attitudes and behaviour will be increasingly shaped by a distorted picture.

But are Christians influenced by what we read and hear in the media? What challenges and opportunities do media narratives around the poor present to us? We will explore these questions in subsequent chapters.

2.5

What shapes our attitudes to poverty?

Having scrutinised almost 400 media articles on poverty in Britain, we turned our attention to finding out what British Christians think about poverty and the poor in our nation. Many of our questions were designed to match or be similar to those asked in other national surveys, particularly the annual British Social Attitudes surveys, so that we would have some comparison data between what Christians think and what members of the public in general think. Our survey ran for three weeks in the summer of 2014 and was completed by 419 people.

We asked a variety of questions: the aim of some was to uncover where we draw the line when it comes to describing someone as 'in need'; with others we were hoping to detect any trends among Christians in terms of blaming the poor for their predicament or factors beyond their control. However, the key thing we wanted to know was how the views of Christians are shaped – we wanted to explore which factors most influence us when it comes to our views on poverty and the poor in Britain today.

Among the headline results, we found that, broadly speaking, Christians have a slightly narrower definition of who is in poverty than the general public, but a very similar outlook when it comes to perceiving that there is 'quite a lot' of poverty in Britain today. However, fewer Christians believe there is 'very little' poverty by a significant margin. In general the respondents in our survey adopted a more sympathetic approach to people on means-tested benefits than the general public. When it came to attitudes about how much support people receive from the State, our results were almost the opposite to those that have been found nationally, with over half of our respondents (54%) believing the level is too low, causing hardship, compared to 22% of the general public believing likewise and 57% stating that they are too high and put people off finding work.[39]

So, Christians seem to be more sympathetic to those in need, more aware of the poverty that exists in Britain, and less prone to buying into myths about people on benefits. But the more important questions we wanted to answer were concerned with how our views are shaped and what influences beliefs about poverty in Britain today. We wanted to know if our opinions are formed by the fact that we are Christians, or if there are other factors at play.

An initial scan of our survey results appeared to show that there were key differences between those in paid church leadership and those with no church leadership role. Curiously, it seemed that our findings were in direct contrast with a comparable survey run by the Church Urban Fund in 2012,[40] where church leaders held softer attitudes towards the poor than their congregations. We wondered if things had changed dramatically in the two-year interval between the CUF survey and ours. Had church members *en masse* caught up with their leaders by becoming persuaded that poverty in Britain is real? Had they realised that it is simply not true that most people on benefits are fiddling the system or want to be dependent on the State? It seems not: when we drilled deeper, we realised that a far more influential factor was political preferences.

This actually translated across all of our questions. In fact, the political party with which respondents most identify caused huge swings in the answers given across the board. From narrow to broad definitions of poverty, to beliefs about those on benefits, to whose responsibility it is to help those in need – the answers fell along the lines of political ideologies. Here are just three examples from the many we could have picked:

- 41% of those who identify with the Conservatives believe there is 'quite a lot' of poverty, compared to 74%, 70% and 66% of those who identify with the Greens, Labour and no party, respectively.

- Likewise, there are political differences among those who answered that there is 'very little' poverty in Britain today: 15% among those most identifying with the Conservatives; 13% Liberal Democrats; two per cent among Labour identifiers; and two per cent among those who do not identify with any political party.

- 33% of those who identify with the Conservatives agree that the income gap between rich and poor is morally wrong compared to 78% Green, 67% Labour, 48% Liberal Democrat and 52% of those not identifying with any political party.

As well as political preferences playing a big role in how people answered our questions, media consumption was a significant factor too. Some might argue that we pick news sources that are broadly in line with our views rather than the media shaping our views. However, few people choose their media based on their views on poverty and generally we are much more influenced by the underlying values of our chosen media than we realise. Biblically, we know that what we read, watch, think about and dwell on matters. Our survey results clearly show that our choice of media and our answers to questions around poverty are intrinsically linked. Again, we could have cited several examples, but here are just three:

- The proportion who believe there is 'quite a lot' of poverty falls from 60% in our survey overall to 49% among regular *Daily Mail* readers and 50% of those who regularly read *The Telegraph* or *The Sun*, but rises to 73% among regular readers of the *Daily Mirror*.

- Media consumption plays a part in the debate about whether large income gaps between the rich and poor are 'morally wrong', with regular readers of the *Daily Mail* (36%), *The Telegraph* (39%) and *The Times* (48%) least likely to agree, and those who regularly read the *Daily Mirror* (73%), *The Sun* (67%), *The Guardian* (65%) and *The Independent* (64%) most likely to agree.

- In assessing the level of help available from the State, 36% of *Daily Mail* readers believe it is not enough, causing hardship, compared to 80% of *Daily Mirror* readers. Over a third of *The Telegraph* and *Daily Mail* readers believe people in need receive enough from the Government; only 13% from the *Daily Mirror* and 14% from the *Huffington Post* believe the same.

Curiously, those who read the newspapers we found to be most sympathetic to the poor are more likely to think media coverage of poverty in Britain 'mostly inaccurate' – 73% of regular *Daily Mirror* readers, 68% of *The Independent* and 63% of *The Guardian*. Conversely, only 33% of *The Sun* readers believe media coverage of poverty is 'mostly inaccurate'.

In addition to political preferences and media consumption influencing our answers, there was a third factor at work: proximity to poverty. We found that people whose employment involves directly helping those in need on a regular basis have far more sympathetic views towards the poor than those who do not regularly help those in need. Again, here are just three examples:

- Of respondents whose work involves helping those in need, five per cent believe Government support is more than enough and 62% believe it is less than enough; of those who do not directly help people in need on a regular basis, 15% answered 'more than enough' and 44% said 'less than enough'.

- 85% of people who work with those in poverty believe everyone deserves help from Christians/ churches, compared to 70% of those who do not regularly help people in need.

- Among those whose work involves helping the poor, 10% believe that faith groups such as churches are primarily responsible for helping people in need, compared to no one among those who do not regularly directly help those in need.

There is a direct correlation between proximity to the poor and the answers chosen in our survey, just as there is a clear connection between people's views on poverty and both political preferences and media consumption.

In general terms, it is interesting to note that half of our respondents (53%) feel that central Government is primarily responsible for helping people in need in Britain, with a further 14% believing it is local government. Only one per cent feels it is primarily for people in poverty to help themselves, and only nine per cent believe faith groups such as churches are primarily responsible. However, while exactly half of our respondents believe everyone in need in Britain deserves help from the Government, a significantly higher proportion (78%) believes everyone in need deserves help from Christians/churches. So there is broad consensus that Christians/churches should not turn away those in need.

The results of our survey present us with a sobering challenge in terms of why we believe what we believe. Where we might expect broad consensus among Christians, we find that our responses to poverty and the poor are divided according to political preferences, media consumption and proximity to those in poverty. The influence of our news sources is a particular concern in light of our media analysis. Are there clear biblical values that should guide us more than what we read or experience? As we now turn our attention to the Bible, hopefully God's perspectives on poverty will begin to influence us more heavily than any other factors.

3

A BIBLICAL
CASE FOR
RADICAL MERCY

THE RELEVANCE OF ANCIENT
ISRAEL'S SOCIAL SYSTEM

Many people find the study of the Law of Moses very uninteresting – and irrelevant. After all, in one sense it has been made redundant by the coming of the gospel. We are no longer under obligation to obey the Mosaic Law, so it is a matter of little interest to most Christians. However, it may not turn out to be as unimportant to us as we first thought. The Law of Moses was designed to create a social system for the nation of Israel. Although its exact provisions are certainly not applicable for today, its underlying ethos and principles help us in other ways.

One example of this is the issue of poverty. The Mosaic Law identified the needs of the poor very clearly and made numerous stipulations in order for them to be both protected and provided for. In essence, the Mosaic Law used the power of the civic authorities to prevent extreme social inequalities. Some examples will demonstrate this: wages had to be paid on time (Leviticus 19:13, Deuteronomy 24:14-15); loans to fellow Israelites were to be without interest (Exodus 22:25, Leviticus 25:36-37); farmers had to leave the edges of their fields un-harvested to enable the poor to glean from them (Leviticus 19:9-10); debts were to be remitted every seven years (Deuteronomy 15:1); and leased land was to be returned to its original owners every 50 years in the Year of Jubilee (Leviticus 25). During the Year of Jubilee, debts were remitted and slaves set free.

There was no direct equivalent to this civic social system in the New Testament because the Church was a different type of community to ancient Israel. It had no single homeland or national identity. It was a Kingdom community, not an ethnic national community. However, Jesus stated that he didn't come to "abolish" the Law of Moses and the Old Testament but to "fulfil" it (Matthew 5:17). Therefore, we would expect to find enduring principles in the Law of Moses concerning the treatment of the poor that have application even after it had run its course and been replaced by the New Covenant. Here are four to consider. Firstly, God is directly interested in the needs of the poor! It's a vital issue to Him. Secondly, the civic authorities have a direct role in helping the poor. Thirdly, the modification of the extremes of wealth and poverty in society is a high priority. Fourthly, God's people should be directly involved in caring for the poor. It's common for Christians to believe that they, as the Church, need to be actively caring for the poor – but it's less common for Christians to be focused on the reasons why the State should also have a significant role.

WHAT CAN WE LEARN FROM THE EXAMPLE OF JESUS?

Jesus is the fulfilment of the story and prophetic direction of the Old Testament. Therefore, any considered response to poverty must focus carefully on the example of Jesus. The wristband slogan 'WWJD' ('What would Jesus do?') is never more relevant than in the case of caring for the poor. The shocking and enthralling fact is that Jesus spent much of his time with those in chronic need and expended a huge amount of emotional and spiritual energy meeting those needs. The Gospel narratives suggest that he quickly got a reputation as a healer and that this drew in vast crowds who followed him around day and night for much of his three years of public ministry (e.g. Mark 3:7-12). Let's take the well known account of the feeding of the 5,000. Why were so many people gathered in a remote place? They were waiting for Jesus to arrive by boat off the Sea of Galilee and were initially seeking healing (Matthew 14:13-14). Once Jesus had healed many of the people, it was well into the afternoon and he either needed to dismiss the crowd to find food in nearby villages or to provide that food himself. He chose to do the latter. But we mustn't forget that it all started with a healing meeting! The Gospel writers are specific in saying that people came from considerable distances and from various different nationalities to receive help from Jesus. On some occasions the crowds were in their thousands rather than their hundreds. No wonder he slipped away on his own from time to time to pray (Luke 5:16) or to take some of his disciples on a quick break from the relentless pressure! (Matthew 15:21)

So why did Jesus spend so much time healing people, releasing them from spiritual oppression, comforting them and miraculously providing for their physical needs? First and foremost, Jesus was motivated by compassion – divine compassion (Matthew 9:36, John 11:33-35). As the Son of God he reflected the character of God accurately in all that he did (Hebrews 1:3). One key aspect of God's character is compassion for the needy and vulnerable. Secondly, it was also part of Jesus' messianic commission to reach out to the poor in both word and deed. The so-called 'Nazareth Manifesto' is explicit:

> *The Spirit of the Lord is on me,*
> *Because he has anointed me*
> *To proclaim good news to the poor.*

> *He has sent me to proclaim freedom for the*
> *prisoners*
> *And recovery of sight for the blind,*
> *To set the oppressed free,*
> *To proclaim the year of the Lord's favour.*
> (Luke 4:18-19)

This dramatic statement, based on Isaiah 61:1-2a, is unambiguous. The 'poor' are the special focus of the ministry of Jesus. In addition, Jesus made it clear that his central work was in announcing that God's Kingdom had arrived, in the sense of being made practical and tangible: "The time has come. The Kingdom of God has come near. Repent and believe the good news!" (Mark 1:15). Jesus came to bring the good news of salvation and he offered his contemporaries the opportunity to have personal faith in him. This was vital to his mission and it is central to the Kingdom message. Jesus is saying that he is the new King and that everyone should come under his rule by believing in what he was doing for them, especially through his death and resurrection. So, with this in mind, where does his care for the poor fit in? Is it a sideshow? No, definitely not. Jesus' care for the poor and his miracles of healing and deliverance were 'signs' of the Kingdom (Luke 11:20) in the sense of revealing the merciful character of God and providing a potential opportunity for the recipients and observers to discover and respond to the full message of the gospel and the coming Kingdom.

Let's sum all this up by taking a look at a famous sequence of events that took place in and around the city of Jericho towards the end of Jesus' life when he was heading to Jerusalem for a final showdown with his opponents. Luke tells the full story (Luke 18:35-19:10). As Jesus approached the city of Jericho, surrounded by a bustling crowd, a blind beggar called out to him: "Jesus, son of David, have mercy on me." Jesus quickly responded and healed the man (and his friend, see Matthew 20:30) – an act of pure mercy. Then, as the crowd pressed in, a local tax collector, Zacchaeus, climbed a tree to see Jesus. Jesus called him down and asked to come to his house. It turns out that Zacchaeus was corrupt and had stolen from many of his fellow citizens. Jesus spoke to him about the Kingdom and he decided to believe in Jesus and turn away from his corruption. He offered to repay all those he had wrongly exploited. Zacchaeus was aware of the healing of the blind men – he may even have seen it. It was a 'sign' to him. Luke's narrative links these two events in a simple and direct way – one followed the other as two demonstrations of God's mercy: Jesus' act of mercy to the blind beggars helped the rich man receive the same mercy and turn from his corrupt life and make a fresh start.

We are left with an intriguing question: did Jesus put any conditions on his acts of mercy and healing? No. He healed all who came to him. The multiplied bread and fish were given to everyone. Jews and Gentiles came to him. Samaritans were not excluded. Men were not favoured above women. Children received special attention. Jesus' mercy seemed to extend across all of humanity. Not everyone responded with gratitude or with faith, but no one was turned away because of who they were or what they had previously been or done.

As we pursue our enquiry into whether the poor can be either deserving or undeserving, we must always keep in mind the challenging and consistent example of Jesus.

BUT SURELY THE POOR WILL ALWAYS BE WITH US?

When Christians discuss poverty it is often not long before someone will quizzically say something like this: "Well, if Jesus said that we're always going to have the poor with us, are we really supposed to get too concerned about it? After all, we can't eradicate poverty, can we?" An interesting half-truth is revealed here. Yes, Jesus did state that poverty would be an ongoing reality in the world (Mark 14:7). He offered no immediate solution to the vast and complex problem of poverty. However, we need to look a little closer at this saying and its context. What Jesus stated was that his followers could only express kindness and generosity to him in person during his life on earth but, by contrast, they will always have the opportunity to express these things to the poor. What a challenge!

DO CHRISTIANS CARE FOR THE POOR WITH STRINGS ATTACHED?

At first glance this seems an easy question to answer from the Bible. There are many texts indicating that love should be unconditional, so it may seem to be obvious that Christians help the poor with no restrictive criteria in mind.

Let's state the case for this position.

We have already noted the extraordinary scope of Jesus' personal acts of mercy towards the poor and needy in his earthly life. There is no sign of Jesus restricting mercy to the poor on the basis of any particular prerequisites or conditions. Interestingly, his teaching bears out the same emphasis. Central to this is the parable of the Good Samaritan, which was really quite revolutionary. Jews of the time understood the

Old Testament command to "love your neighbour as yourself" (Leviticus 19:18) as primarily (if not exclusively) about how they dealt with fellow Jews in local communities. Little did Jesus' questioner in Luke 10:25-29 know what a radical redefinition of loving one's neighbour Jesus was going to make when he was asked: "And who is my neighbour?" The parable that followed overturned Jewish prejudice and culture completely. The Samaritan traveller turned out to be the good guy, while the devout Jews failed the test of love. Jesus' new definition of loving one's neighbour crossed all social distinctions and was universal in application. If this is the case, can there be any conditions placed on acts of mercy?

Jesus is even more challenging when he teaches on loving our enemies in Luke 6:27-36 (see also Matthew 5:43-48). Christians are called to do good even to those who oppose them and seek to exploit their generosity and open-heartedness. If we are called to be "merciful" to the "ungrateful and wicked" (Luke 6:35-36), then surely that implies that we cannot label the poor as undeserving when they approach us for help?

Another reflection is important here. God's mercy came to us initially when we were literally undeserving. We were all sinners. We couldn't do anything to earn the mercy of the gospel. It was literally a free gift to the undeserving. This is the reality of the way unregenerate mankind first encounters the living God and his gospel. If this is the case with personal salvation, then why should it be any different in the way the Church reaches out to the world? If we offer the gospel to those who don't 'deserve' its benefits, then surely we will show mercy to the poor on the same basis?

So the case for unconditional mercy is easily made. Let's now see if there are any biblical arguments that modify this perspective. Two passages from Paul's letters come to mind in this context.

In 2 Thessalonians 3, Paul warns the church against an attitude of idleness. Christian discipleship, according to Paul, involves diligence and a willingness to work hard in all areas of life (verses 6-15). Paul is especially concerned about those who are unwilling to work to earn a living for themselves. He quotes with approval something he had previously discussed with them: "The one who is unwilling to work shall not eat" (verse 10). What does this mean? It seems to be an instruction to the church members to allow the lazy person to experience the consequences of his actions in refusing to work. Paul doesn't want them to bail him out with free meals and cash gifts when he needs to learn to take responsibility for his own life.

Then, in 1 Timothy 5:3-16, Paul addresses the sensitive pastoral question of how to care most appropriately for widows within the congregation at Ephesus. He is seeking to help the church leaders identify real economic need. Firstly, he places the primary responsibility on the individual's family rather than the local church. Then he encourages the church leaders only to help those widows who are genuinely without alternative means of support and are living responsibly.

At face value, passages such as these put definite conditions on the support of church members who are in need. How are we to explain the creative tension that seems to exist between these Pauline statements on the one hand and the teaching and example of Jesus on the other?

It's worth starting by remembering that Paul's overall commitment to care for the poor was central to his ministry. He made clear his determination to "remember the poor" in a discussion about his ministry with the apostles Peter, James and John (Galatians 2:7-10). He then worked hard to put this principle into practice by raising money for impoverished churches (2 Corinthians 8 & 9). We also need to keep in mind the strong emphasis on sharing within the Church community that is frequently described in the pages of the New Testament. The Early Church in Jerusalem is a striking example (e.g. Acts 2:42-47). Paul also emphasised that 'doing good' was not just about Christians helping other Christians in need. Rather, he called the Church "as we have opportunity, to do good to all people…" But then he emphasised that, for the sake of integrity and consistency, the Church should make sure its own needy people are cared for, identifying as a focus "…especially those who belong to the faith" (Galatians 6:10).

In comparing Jesus and Paul it is important to remember that the focus of Jesus' teaching and example was principally based on the initial encounter between those in need and the people of God. In this context, unconditional mercy and help was granted with no questions asked. Paul, however, is often addressing established Christians who have been the recipients of the unconditional mercy of God through the gospel. They now believe and are part of the Church. It seems that they then have to take some measure of responsibility for the conduct of their lives in the light of the unconditional mercy they have previously received. Those who didn't fancy doing a proper job were failing to live out the moral standards of their discipleship.

Likewise, widows who lived self-indulgent lives were wasting the resources they really needed to fund their future lives. It is noteworthy that these unemployed idlers and careless widows were not disenfranchised from the Church. They still had the benefits of the community. It is just that they were not encouraged to continue in unhelpful lifestyles by being propped up by handouts from church leaders or fellow church members.

So where does this leave us? There are several insights that need to be linked together to help us in our discussion.

Firstly, God is merciful. God's initial dealings with those in need are always characterised by unconditional mercy. This may come through the gospel message, through the sacrificial love and friendship of Christians, or through the mercy ministries of the Church. Likewise, our initial encounters with people in need should also be characterised first and foremost by mercy. We mustn't slip into the temptation to ask people to change before we help them. That is a deeply unbiblical response. Our default response should be mercy first.

Secondly, in God's mercy, he wants to bring real change to people's lives. In the case of the poor, this means giving them hope for the future and the knowledge that their lives have value and meaning. It also means giving them increased responsibility for their own lives alongside practical support as the Church engages with their real life situations. This process means that those receiving help never become undeserving in a definitive sense. It means, rather, that our merciful love for them will be expressed in a wider context than initial emergency relief as time goes on. That wider context will seek to enable them to take responsibility for change in their lives so that they do not become enslaved in dependence to a specific form of initial practical help.

As we see in chapter four, some sectors of our contemporary secular society are quick to label some of the poor as undeserving because they may have abused the support of the State or charities. This label has the effect of severing our sense of relationship with and responsibility for such people. It puts them outside the focus of our mercy and care.

The biblical approach is different. For Christians, mercy is engaging with the whole person – not just with the immediate need. There is no cut-off point when they become undeserving. We start with unconditional help, but then seek to engage in the longer term process of bringing dignity and restoration to the poor. This will involve much more than handouts. It will engage with the whole person over time and may well mean that we sometimes decide that ongoing handouts are not in the best interests of specific people. If this is the case, it is only because there is a better way of helping them. It is not because they have become the undeserving poor.

THE HEART BEHIND
THE LABEL UNDESERVING

The parables of Jesus tend to be subversive and often carry hidden depths of meaning that help us to understand various aspects of God's Kingdom. The parable of the workers in the vineyard from Matthew 20:1-16 is a relevant example:

> *For the kingdom of heaven is like a landowner who went out early in the morning to hire workers for his vineyard. He agreed to pay them a denarius for the day and sent them into his vineyard.*

About nine in the morning he went out and saw others standing in the market-place doing nothing. He told them, "You also go and work in my vineyard, and I will pay you whatever is right." So they went.

He went out again about noon and about three in the afternoon and did the same thing. About five in the afternoon he went out and found still others standing around. He asked them, "Why have you been standing here all day long doing nothing?"

"Because no one has hired us," they answered.

He said to them, "You also go and work in my vineyard."

When evening came, the owner of the vineyard said to his foreman, "Call the workers and pay them their wages, beginning with the last ones hired and going on to the first."

The workers who were hired about five in the afternoon came and each received a denarius. So when those came who were hired first, they expected to receive more. But each one of them also received a denarius. When they received it, they began to grumble against the landowner. "These who were hired last worked only one hour," they said, "and you have made them equal to us who have borne the burden of the work and the heat of the day."

But he answered one of them, "Friend, I am not being unfair to you. Didn't you agree to work for a denarius? Take your pay and go. I want to give the one who was hired last the same as I gave you. Don't I have the right to do what I want with my own money? Or are you envious because I am generous?"

So the last will be first, and the first will be last.

This is a rather shocking story. The outline is clear but the outcomes are surprising. The scene was a commonplace one in the Israel of Jesus' day. Much agricultural labouring was done on a short-term basis. Men looking for employment tended to gather in village market places. These were the poor of their time. They generally had no land of their own and would be unemployed unless someone offered them work. Some were keener to work than others: some arrived early at the market and pushed themselves forward to work; others were less punctual and less determined.

In this story the owner of the vineyard offered those who worked all day a fair wage for a day's work – one denarius. But interestingly, he never told the subsequently hired workers exactly what their wage would be – only that it would be "right". So when he paid all the workers exactly the same wage at the end of the day, he could honestly say that he had given the workers what he had promised, even though it was not strictly according to the hours that they had worked. This did not stop those who had worked all day putting in a strongly worded complaint about the injustice of the situation!

What's so significant about this challenging and unusual story? Firstly, the focus is on the owner and his unusual attitude towards the unemployed, including those whose credentials in terms of attitude and focus could be questioned. He did not reject those who hadn't bothered to show up when he first visited the marketplace. He went back to look out for them several times during the day and gave them a genuine hand-up by employing them on generous terms part way through the day. His motive seems to be compassion for the poor. Secondly, the issue of contention at the end of the story revolves around the inability of the more diligent workers to understand that grace was being extended to the other workers who had worked for less of the day. The compassion and grace of the owner provoked uproar!

Jesus wanted his listeners to identify something of God the Father's attitudes in those of the owner of the vineyard. Just as the owner was compassionate and generous to the poor, so we are called upon to have the same type of attitude. There is no cut-off point for the compassionate engagement of the owner with the poor – he makes no moralistic distinctions between them. This parable shines a sharp and uncomfortable light on the current tendency to label some as the undeserving poor.

Section 4

WHO ARE
THE POOR?

Identifying who are the poor can seem complex in the context of media framing the debate by pitting 'strivers' against 'skivers' – the hard-working, decent folk against those who are quite comfortable being supported by the State and even revel in it. Extremes of each stereotype are regularly wheeled out to make ideological points: the 'characters' of *Benefits Street* versus the 'cast' of *Breadline Kids*; the 'guilty' whose moral failings are to blame for their poverty compared with the innocent poor children missing meals. These ubiquitous images perpetuate the notion that some of the poor are deserving of help and some are undeserving.

For those of us living in Britain today, how we identify who are the poor can be highly subjective and, as we have seen, is influenced by the media, political preferences and our proximity to those in poverty. We live at a time in which television images of starving, water-deprived, malnourished children in Third World countries are haunting but commonplace; similar images of hungry children in Britain are increasing but are not as familiar to us. Views of poverty handed to us by the media are selective, agenda-driven (whether that's by the media outlet or the advertiser) snapshots that do not tell the whole, complex, nuanced story, and do not necessarily reflect the varied types of poverty identified in the Bible. They can lead us to ask the question: is anyone in modern-day Britain truly poor?

How we answer this question is of crucial importance: it will not only shape our attitudes, but also our actions. There are many different ways in which we can identify who is in poverty in Britain today. In our survey, definitions of poverty were wide-ranging, including:

"It's relative and mostly spiritual and aspirational."

"People unable to afford life's essentials or unable to afford them without anxiety."

"Exclusion from society due to lack of money."

"Those who are in poverty or poor in Britain are labelled scroungers and lazy, but poverty is defined by life opportunities and the unfair and unequal distribution of wealth."

"Poor education regarding options and potential for young people. Lack of father figures/examples."

"Poverty is being unable to provide for my basic needs and have no initiative to remedy my situation."

"Surviving hand to mouth, but with no savings to help during a rainy day, no advocacy to plead your cause to those in power, no education to help you better yourself and no hope that things could ever get better."

Many of these descriptions of poverty are much broader than the Government's, which draws a line relative to average earnings, defining relative poverty as those households in which the income is less than 60% of the median national income. However, the limitations of a purely economic definition are acknowledged by the Government – the Minister responsible for the most sweeping welfare reforms since the 1940s, Iain Duncan Smith, concedes: "Across the UK, there are children living in circumstances that simply cannot be captured by assessing whether their household has more or less than 60% of the average income. There are many factors that impact on a child's wellbeing and ability to succeed in life."[41]

However, even in our own survey, half of the Christian respondents (51%) selected the narrowest definition of poverty from three available options, which stated that "someone in Britain is in poverty if they have not got enough to eat and live without getting into debt". Only 12% of Christians picked the broadest option of "...if they have enough to buy all the things they really need, but not enough to buy the things most people take for granted". Obviously we are still talking in terms of economic poverty here but, according to leading UK research institute Ipsos MORI, the reality in Britain today is that "whichever way poverty is defined, some believe that those who are in this state are there by choice or because of their own poor decision-making and, more generally, that there is a distinction between the deserving and undeserving poor".[42]

How are Christians to tackle this issue? Our survey findings revealed that politics and media consumption heavily influence our views on poverty and the poor in Britain. Therefore, our starting place with the question of 'who are the poor?' has to be analysing our own hearts, attitudes and prejudices to see whether or not we square up with the biblical narrative – with God's perspective. The Bible doesn't present poverty as a one-dimensional, purely economical issue, but as nuanced and multi-faceted. The framework it gives us for answering 'who are the poor?' has four distinct elements:

- Economic poverty – lacking the material means to support themselves to live viably within our society;
- Relational poverty – lacking a family or community support network to which they can turn in troubled times (family breakdown is a key issue here);
- Aspirational poverty – lacking hope or capacity to extricate themselves from the situation they are in;

- Spiritual poverty – not knowing "the God of our Lord Jesus Christ, the glorious Father" (Ephesians 1:17).[43]

The Old Testament addresses itself to the identity of the poor very specifically. There is a reason for this. Israel was constituted as a nation state once it had entered into the promised land of Canaan. God had already given Moses the terms of the legal system that was designed to be used to govern the people in the land. An obvious issue in this context was dealing with the poor. Common descriptions of those in poverty in the Law of Moses were "widows", "fatherless", "foreigners" and "the poor" (see, for example, Leviticus 19:10 & 15, 23:22, Deuteronomy 10:18, 14:29, 24:17-21). These were the main categories of the socially disadvantaged in their society. The widows and fatherless had no one to protect and provide for them. Foreigners were social outsiders without any landholding, and the poor were those who had fallen on hard times either through their own actions or, more commonly, through misfortune or the abuse of power by others. The prophets used this description of the poor as a summary of poverty in ancient Israel. They were clear that it was the duty of all Israelites, especially the rulers, to care for the poor:

> *This is what the Lord Almighty said:*
> *Administer true justice;*
> *Show mercy and compassion to one another.*
> *Do not oppress the widow or the fatherless, the foreigners or the poor.*
> *Do not plot evil against one another.*
> (Zechariah 7:10)

From a biblical point of view, the poor are first and foremost those who, for whatever reason, are unable to support themselves economically in order to live viably within the society in which they live. Nevertheless, the biblical framework for poverty is broader than economic poverty – other types of poverty are included in several passages of Scripture. For example, in Isaiah 58 we read that the kind of fasting God desires from his people benefits victims of injustice, those who are oppressed, the hungry, the homeless, and the naked. These might be predominantly facing economic poverty. Three chapters later, in the verses quoted by Jesus at the start of his ministry (see Luke 4:18-19), the broken-hearted, the captive, the prisoner, and the mourner are added in. These may be in economic poverty too, but they are likely to be struggling with either relational poverty or aspirational poverty or both as well. Looking back to the Mosaic Law, we see those in debt and those enslaved included (Deuteronomy 15), as are widows, orphans, the fatherless, and foreigners (Exodus 22) and the lonely (Psalm 68) – again, a mix of economic, relational and aspirational poverty can be detected. If it seems that God's Old Testament definition of who poverty affects is very broad, wait until we get to Jesus!

Through the gospels we see many poor and needy people come to Jesus. We also see Jesus go to the poor and needy. He ate at the home of Simon the Leper – not a nickname that would attract most of us into someone's house, let alone to the dinner table. He mixed with and made time for people from all walks of life and didn't consider anyone 'beneath' him. Those on the margins of society – shunned beggars, 'unclean' lepers, shamed prostitutes and despised tax collectors – not only felt comfortable around him, but actively sought him out and wanted to spend time with him. Jesus reached out to those who were despised and marginalised – to those who were poor economically, relationally, aspirationally and spiritually. When it came to dispensing mercy, Jesus viewed the tax collector as just as needy as those begging on the streets, because Jesus knew that the tax collector was relationally poor, lacking a community who cared for and supported him, even though he may be economically rich.

The reasons for these various types of poverty are often not described specifically or explicitly in the biblical accounts of the poor. However, there are a number of explanations for poverty given consistently throughout the Bible or implicit in the stories. Let's have a look at those reasons.

A central reason for poverty is that some people become the victims of deliberate exploitation by others. Injustice and oppression divide society into the 'haves' and 'have nots'. This was as true in biblical times as it is today and needs to be prevented (e.g. Exodus 21:22-27). It was a constant concern of the Old Testament prophets (e.g. Amos 2:6-8), John the Baptist (e.g. Luke 3:10-14), Jesus (e.g. Luke 16:19-31) and the apostles (e.g. James 5:1-6). As the income gap between the rich and the poor dramatically increases in Britain today, this needs to be our concern, too.

A second reason often given is through natural disasters. The seven years of drought in ancient Egypt caused intense suffering to the Egyptian people and Joseph was raised up as a political leader to alleviate these difficulties through food distribution (Genesis 41). Locust swarms devastated Israel in the days of Joel (Joel

1 & 2) and famine ravaged the Roman world in the days of the Early Church (Acts 11:27-30). We may think this reason is not so relevant in Britain today, but we need look no further than those who have been forced out of their homes due to flooding in recent years than to see this is still a cause of hardship of which Christians need to be aware.

The third reason for poverty is what one might call accidental. Jesus describes the fate of those who happened to be under a tower when it fell over unexpectedly to illustrate that accidents do just happen. The victims are not morally worse than those who escape – they just happened to be in the wrong place at the wrong time (Luke 13:4). For example, we know that Jesus healed many lepers and we also know that many people in those days contracted the disease accidentally.

The final reason given for poverty is also important. The Bible makes clear that some people are poor through their own wrong actions. They bring it upon themselves. The book of Proverbs emphasises this point, noting, for example, the danger of laziness (Proverbs 6:7-11) and the lure of living above one's means (Proverbs 21:17).

Just as we see in the Bible, people in 21st century Britain can find themselves in economic poverty because of injustice, accidents or other circumstances beyond their control, or through their own mistakes or bad choices. Likewise, relational poverty and aspirational poverty can also come about for a variety of reasons. The reality for many people in need is that they will be affected by more than one of these types of poverty, perhaps in terms of both cause and effect. For example, family breakdown has been highlighted as one of 'five pathways to poverty' by the Centre for Social Justice[44]

– the relational poverty that can emerge from family breakdown can have a huge bearing on economic and aspirational poverty. In the biblical references to different types of people who are poor, the call on God's people never seems dependent on how the person got into poverty in the first place or what type of poverty they are in, but rather depends on who God is and what he values: mercy, justice, kindness and compassion.

When we hear stories of people such as 39-year-old Tom, who can't feed his 14-year-old daughter Niomi and his 12-year-old son Drey because he gave up his job when Niomi was diagnosed with leukaemia, and who can't claim Job Seekers' Allowance because he can't look for work,[45] the instinctive response from most of us will be sympathy and compassion. It's very different when we hear of someone who says they'd rather live on benefits because they're better off that way, and they can get a bigger house by having more kids – our sympathy and compassion quickly erode, often replaced instantly by a sense of outrage.

But this misses the point about different types of poverty. It sets a cut-off point for our compassion, failing to take into account that the person who doesn't want to work is also in a type of poverty – probably aspirational and spiritual. In so much of the current analyses of child poverty in Britain today, we discover the odds stacked against poor children becoming anything other than poor adults. In fact, poverty has the biggest influence on the chances they will have in life.[46] They are less likely to do well at school, less likely to have aspirations for the future, less likely to be healthy and more likely to die prematurely, less likely to have a well paid job when they are adults.[47] At what age do we switch off our compassion towards these children and turn it into outrage towards them for not making better decisions in life? It is illogical to expect children in poverty who are facing such bleak outcomes to suddenly, at some point on the road to adulthood, be transformed into grown-ups who bear no resemblance to the circumstances in which they grew up. Yet for many of us there comes a point at which a deserving poor child becomes an undeserving poor adult.

The types of poverty we see in the Bible are not limited to material or physical needs, but encompass those who have no power to change their circumstances and no hope of improving their lot. Those who cannot meet their own needs – whether that is because they cannot afford food (economic poverty) or because they have no experience of the dignity and worth that comes from earning a living and therefore do not want to work (aspirational poverty) – are the poor. Poverty is not just about money; Jesus "went around doing good" (Acts 10:38) to those who were in physical need but also to those who were hopeless, mourning, oppressed and despised – to those who were relationally, aspirationally and spiritually poor, as well as economically.

Jesus calls us to be radically different to those around us, not just in our actions, but also in our attitudes. He puts it in crystal clear – and deeply challenging – terms in Luke 14:12-14:

> *When you give a luncheon or dinner, do not invite your friends, your brothers or relatives, or your rich neighbours; if you do, they may invite you back and so you will be repaid. But when you give a banquet, invite the poor, the crippled, the lame,*

the blind, and you will be blessed. Although they cannot repay you, you will be repaid at the resurrection of the righteous.

The Message version puts it like this: *"Don't just invite... the kind of people who will return the favour. Invite some people who never get invited out, the misfits from the wrong side of the tracks."*

This is a striking command from Jesus about how his followers are to interact with those who 'are not like them', around whom they may naturally feel uncomfortable. Sometimes the people we most want to avoid are the very ones God is seeking out. And when it comes to poverty, he puts the onus on us: we are to look out for and invite those who are poor, hurting, broken or lonely and show kindness, compassion and friendship, without expecting anything in return. After all, this is exactly how Jesus has treated us! We were enemies of God when Jesus died for us. We were once sinners, outside of God's family and Kingdom, with nothing to offer him by which we might gain entry, and with no case by which we could plead for his mercy. Yet he lavished it on us anyway, because the nature of mercy is that it has nothing to do with the recipient and everything to do with the one being merciful.

In the foodbank my (Natalie) church runs, we see people come for help for all sorts of reasons, from a bereaved widow who could not feed her children, to a woman who described herself as "previously very well-off" until her business suddenly folded leaving her "practically destitute". We see victims of domestic violence and large families whose benefits have been changed, delayed or stopped. We see people who have racked up debt to pay the bills and young, single people who cannot find jobs. We see people who are sick and people who have lived beyond their means. We give food to all who come, and look for ways to help beyond that if we can.

Jesus dealt wisely with all who came to him – sometimes he tested their hearts, for example, asking if they really wanted to be healed or refusing to perform a miracle on demand – but he didn't deal with people on a deserving or undeserving basis: he responded to people on an individual level but always on the basis of his mercy, not their worthiness. When we read the accounts of Jesus feeding the 4,000 and the 5,000, there is no mention of the disciples means-testing the crowds, weeding out those who were just there for a free meal or those who should have known better than to come out without a packed lunch. This doesn't mean that we should help everyone who asks without finding out something about their circumstances, but it does mean that our motivation for asking should not be so we can judge them as deserving or undeserving. Instead, it should only be so that we can more effectively help each person in need with the real problem and the root causes.

It is true that poverty can be the result of sin or folly – we have seen that in the Bible. However, even when sin is to blame for someone's poverty, our attitude should not be a worldly 'you made your bed, now lie in it' but instead we know that just as we can help with economic poverty, we are also those who carry the answer to spiritual poverty. We may not approve of people's behaviour; we may believe there is a better way to live. But Jesus has never treated us according to our behaviour – he treats us according to who we are, which is people made in the image of God, created to know him and reflect him to those around us. That is why, when Jesus saw the crowds, "he had compassion on them, because they were harassed and helpless, like sheep without a shepherd" (Matthew 9:36).

When you see the crowds – whether it's face-to-face or in the media – how do you feel about them?

DEVELOPING A HEART FOR THE POOR

When I (Natalie) moved to China for a year's work placement, I was instructed early on not to give money to children begging in the street. The first time I ignored this, I found out why: giving even the smallest amount of money to a child would immediately mean being surrounded by literally dozens, with as many as could cling onto you doing exactly that until you couldn't move. Sometimes, though, compassion would compel me to give, even knowing what would happen as a result. Late one night, I bought a small rice cake and gave it to an excessively skinny, dirty child wearing filthy, threadbare rags. I watched him run off with it and, to my surprise, hand it to a woman – his mother, I assumed. She was wearing dirty clothes too, but was wrapped up in more layers. I watched as she broke off a small piece of the rice cake, probably less than a tenth of it. I presumed she would give the rest back to the boy, but instead she passed him the small piece and ate the larger portion herself. I was outraged! In that moment, I thought: "I would never have bought food for the boy if I'd known what his mother would do!"

It wasn't until years later that, when telling this story, a different thought occurred to me: "How desperately hungry would a woman have to be to deprive her child of food?" But what happened in my heart in the middle of the night on the streets of Beijing was not a rise of compassion or kindness or generosity or mercy, but a flash of judgment and anger and an instant categorisation of the woman as undeserving of my help. And I didn't feel bad about that at all – it seemed an entirely justified and normal response. Being honest, I think that today, as I've just typed this story, is the first time I've felt deeply ashamed of my heart's knee-jerk reaction.

How about you? What happens in your heart when you pass someone begging in the street? What about when they're holding a cigarette or feeding their dog? How do you react when someone turns up to a church meeting at 10am reeking of alcohol for the fifth week in a row, asking for money for food? Or when the conversation turns to immigration or welfare reform or someone on benefits with eight children?

Observing what happens in our hearts when we come into contact with poverty is vitally important if we are to reflect the heart of the Father to those in need and to be more like Jesus in both our attitudes and actions. We won't respond to poverty with the compassion and mercy Jesus showed the poor if our hearts are hard. We see in the Bible that God's displeasure with humankind and his own people is so often inextricably connected to their treatment of the poor, vulnerable and marginalised in society. We have seen in previous chapters that there is a very real danger that we Christians can have our attitudes shaped as much by political preferences and media consumption as by biblical values – perhaps even more so! But the Gospel demands more of us: the children of God are called not to fit in with the dominant attitudes of the culture around them, but to stand out – to "shine like stars in the universe as you hold out the word of life" (Philippians 2:15). The norm in our society is to respond to people according to their behaviour; the norm for the Christian is to have fixed values that do not move according to someone else's behaviour but are rooted in how only one person behaved: Jesus Christ. The biblical values that will help us in our attitudes towards the poor in Britain today relate to people, truth, kindness, mercy, justice and generosity. Let's explore each one in turn.

PEOPLE

Our attitudes towards people in poverty (and people in general) can so often be based on the things they say and do, but our starting place should always be that every single person is created in the image of God, known by him and loved by him. This immediately gives each individual dignity and worth. This needs to be the first and uppermost thought in our minds and hearts when we encounter people in poverty, whether that's face-to-face, in conversations or through our newspapers or televisions. Our perceptions of people must honour the stamp of the Creator in them. We may not like someone's behaviour or their attitude, but that shouldn't affect our behaviour or attitude towards them. Our attitudes must be rooted in honouring the value God places on every person.

Therefore, even if we think the system, structures or institutions are flawed, we mustn't write off entire groups of people or even individuals. God doesn't; each one is crafted in his image and dearly loved by him. This first value alone does not give the Christian much room for making judgments about the deserving and the undeserving poor. How can any person who is made in the image of God, loved by him, but in need, be undeserving of our help? Of course, the nature of that help will differ from person to person, according to their unique situation – there is often a fine line between helping someone out of poverty and helping someone to remain in poverty – but the attitudes of our hearts should be grounded in God's heart for those he has made.

TRUTH

Truth is extremely important to Christians. Jesus came full of truth and proclaimed that he is the truth, that the truth sets us free, and that the Holy Spirit would come to guide us into all truth (John 1:14, 14:6, 8:32, 16:13 respectively). Obviously this is the truth that Jesus is the Son of God and that he died on the cross, paying for our sins, and rose again that we may have eternal life with him. But it would be erroneous of us to think – consciously or unconsciously – that a Christian need only be concerned with the truth of the gospel and not with truth in general. One of the Ten Commandments given to Moses for the people of God was: "You shall not give false testimony against your neighbour" (Exodus 20:16), followed by: "Do not spread false reports..." (23:1). Furthermore, "the righteous hate what is false" (Proverbs 13:5) and the apostle Paul commanded Christians "do not lie to each other, since you have taken off your old self with its practices and have put on the new self, which is being renewed in knowledge in the image of its Creator" (Colossians 3:9-10).

Christians have a responsibility to stand up for truth not just when it is *the* truth of the gospel, but also for truth in general. One of the great ironies of the age of technology is that with so much information at the click of a button or the swipe of a screen, it is increasingly difficult to find out the truth about certain issues. This is true of information about poverty, which is vast and easily accessible, yet so often manipulated to reinforce a particular ideology or belief.

In the 2013 report we mentioned earlier, *The Lies We Tell Ourselves: Ending Comfortable Myths About Poverty*, the authors sought to expose seven of the most commonly perpetuated myths about the poor in Britain. The report attempted to dismantle lies such as most of the poor "are lazy and don't want to work", "are addicted to drink and drugs", and "are on the fiddle" by quoting alternative facts and figures, which are startling in their contrast to the dominant narratives we read and hear. "It can be comforting to believe poverty mainly visits those who deserve it," they wrote, even if there is significant evidence in the opposite direction.

When Christians think or talk about poverty in Britain, we must not let our minds lazily leap to stereotypes, to examples on the extreme ends of the spectrum, or to pithy but ill-conceived soundbites. When we do this, our mouths perpetuate myths, our hearts become hardened and our hands hang limply in inaction. Wherever we stand politically, whatever our experience of poverty, whichever media we consume – we are called to care about what is true. This means we should be those who work hard to get the reality of statistics and stories – or we should keep quiet until we have. This is especially the case with the poor, who are mostly 'voiceless' when it comes to power, influence and media presence. If those in the midst of poverty cannot speak out about the truth of their experiences and the injustices they suffer, Christians must passionately care about exposing myths and standing up for truth.

KINDNESS

Jesus was incredibly kind to everyone he encountered. It didn't mean watering down his words, but it did mean reaching out to those around him and healing, feeding, accepting, releasing, teaching and loving them. God never withholds his goodness from us (regardless of how we respond to it) and likewise we're not to withhold kindness and goodness from those with whom we come into contact. Our default setting should be to show kindness to the poor, regardless of who they are and how they got there. Proverbs says: "The poor are shunned even by their neighbours, but the rich have many friends. He who despises his neighbour sins, but blessed is he who is kind to the needy... whoever is kind to the needy honours God" (Proverbs 14:20-21 & 31). And therein lays the crux of an attitude of kindness: rather than looking to the causes of poverty or the specific details of the plight of the poor, it looks to honour God by showing the same kindness that he has shown.

Doing good feels good because it is good! It is one of the things we were created to do. Kindness, compassion, generosity – these are things that were always supposed to come naturally to us. It's a mark of how far humanity has fallen that often our hearts default to responses that are the exact opposite and can even feel more 'normal' to us.

We can often think of kindness as an action, and to have meaning it must translate into action, but if the attitude of our hearts is not kindness, we won't act kindly. A kind heart wants to do good to those in poverty – it spots a need and is eager to help. When it sees a father with small children at the supermarket checkout putting a few items aside due to lack of money, the attitude of a kind heart isn't impatience at being held up in the queue, but is motivated to reach a hand into a wallet and make a difference. When it sees someone begging on the streets, it doesn't motivate our legs to cross the road but our mouths to ask if there is anything we can do to help. An act of kindness is a beautiful thing to behold precisely because it reveals a heart of compassion – a heart like God's.

MERCY

Mercy strikes at the very heart of any categorisation of the poor as deserving or undeserving because mercy is, by its very nature, always undeserved. That's the point of it. A merciful attitude is one that says, "Even if I could legitimately say you don't deserve my help, I'm going to help you anyway." It is God's attitude towards us: he has not treated us as we deserve; he has done the exact opposite. He has not asked us to earn his mercy by contributing something towards it – the only thing we contribute is all our heaps of sin! Yet we so often expect more from those around us, and this attitude can so easily creep into our perceptions of the poor in Britain today.

When we look to Jesus, though, we are left with no option but to cultivate a heart of mercy. Almost everything Jesus did was an act of mercy: he fed vast crowds because he could see that they were hungry; he calmed raging seas because the disciples were afraid; he turned water into wine to spare the bridegroom's shame.

These stories are often thought of as signs of the power of God, but each one was an act of mercy too. What's more, they bore no relation to behaviour – Jesus bestowed mercy liberally, regardless of how the recipient would respond. For example, in Luke 17 we find Jesus healed 10 men but only one returned to express gratitude. We don't go on to read that Jesus revoked the healings from the other nine or chased after them! Jesus said: "But love your enemies, do good to them, and lend to them without expecting anything back. Then your reward will be great, and you will be sons of the Most High, because he is kind to the ungrateful and wicked. Be merciful, just as your Father is merciful" (Luke 6:35-36). Jesus was merciful because it was in his nature to be merciful. Christians are imitators of Christ, being transformed to become more and more like him. Therefore, our hearts need to become increasingly merciful too.

JUSTICE

God is a God of justice. The Bible tells us that he always does what is right; it is littered with verses declaring that he absolutely abhors injustice. This means that his children are to love justice and hate injustice too. What does a heart that loves justice look like? In relation to the poor, it seeks for them to not be disadvantaged due to lack of wealth or status, but to be elevated, valued and given a voice. A heart that loves justice longs "to loose the chains of injustice" (Isaiah 58:6) – chains that lock people into their situations and restrict their opportunities (or even their aspirations) to improve their lot – and to "do away with the yoke of oppression, with the finger pointing and malicious talk" (verse 9).

In today's Britain, an attitude of justice for the poor is radical and counter-cultural because it refuses to buy into the myth that some people deserve help and some do not, and it turns away from "finger pointing and malicious talk" that accuses the poor and blames them, seeing poverty as a moral failure or character defect. It does away with any notion of superiority of the rich and inferiority of the poor, recognising that there are many factors leading to wealth and status (or lack thereof) and several have nothing to do with deserving or not deserving what one has. Instead, a heart for justice concerns itself with finding out the reality of the situation, standing up for those in need, and looking for ways to lift people out of poverty. Justice brings together many of the aspects we have looked at in this chapter, because it cares about truth, it recognises that there is a story behind each individual's situation, and then compels us into merciful and kind action.

GENEROSITY

Finally, unlike my response to the woman in Beijing who ate most of the rice cake, Christian attitudes to the poor should be shaped by generosity of heart. In Deuteronomy 15, God tells his people "do not be hard-hearted or tight-fisted" (verse 7) but that can so easily be our response to poverty in Britain today. We can quickly ask questions about the circumstances surrounding a person's poverty – there's nothing wrong with this per se, but we must watch our hearts to see if we are asking so we can attribute blame or worthiness to receive help. We can sometimes dress this up as 'being responsible' or 'due diligence', which are important, but if we are honest with ourselves and with God, we can often recognise that our hearts are carrying an attitude of hardness or tight-fistedness rather than one of mercy and generosity.

Like kindness, if our hearts aren't flooded with an attitude of generosity, we are unlikely to be generous. We can so easily buy into the beliefs of our culture, which would tell us that what we have is ours, we earned it and we deserve it, rather than the biblical perspective that all we have is a gift from God, unmerited and to be at his disposal. The ideology of 'the American dream' is pervasive in Britain too: it tells us that we can all have more than enough if we just work hard enough.

But that is not the reality for many of the poor in Britain today, who are working but keep falling further behind. It should trouble us deeply that the gap between the rich and the poor is growing fast in Britain.[48] It exposes the myth that our wealth and status is built predominantly on 'karma', and highlights the need for us all to adopt a generous attitude towards those in need.

Christians can set our benchmark at giving away a tithe (10%) of what we earn, but what God calls us to is a heart that overflows with generosity because he has been so overwhelmingly generous with us. This, too, is radically counter-cultural. It is an attitude that does not accept that it is ok for us to have much more than we need while there are people in our communities who have much less than they need. We are called to imitate Jesus in putting the interests of others above our own (see Philippians 2:1-11).

A BIBLICAL ATTITUDE

Our attitudes towards the poor are shaped in a number of ways. In the survey we conducted in the summer of 2014, we found that political preferences and media consumption contribute strongly to the way we think about poverty in Britain today. The easy route is to swallow the dominant narratives of the day and regurgitate whichever of them suits our particular ideologies. We also found that proximity to those in poverty plays a vital part in how we think, and this can be helpful in cultivating increased sympathy and empathy towards those in need, as we shall see in the next chapter.

Christians, though, are to be shaped primarily and predominantly by what God thinks about the poor, and what God thinks is abundantly clear through the Scriptures. We must allow the narrative of the Bible to have the loudest volume and the largest space in our hearts and minds, even when it means dramatic shifts of attitude need to take place.

The actions of Christians in alleviating poverty in Britain today send a strong message to Government, the media, local decision-makers, the general public and the poor themselves, but it is vitally important that our attitudes at the very least match up – and at best propel us into greater good works. "Out of the overflow of the heart the mouth speaks" (Matthew 12:34) so let our hearts be shaped not by cultural values nor by media narratives nor by political ideologies nor even by our own experiences. Instead, may the attitudes of our hearts increasingly be moulded by the biblical values of people, truth, kindness, mercy, justice and generosity, which are vitally important. When these values are embedded in our hearts, it becomes impossible for us to believe the myth of the undeserving poor.

Section 6

A CALL TO ACTION

Facing up to poverty and raw human need is a complex business. It challenges our culture, lifestyle, busyness, assumptions and comfort zones. Some Christians get angry and defensive when poverty comes knocking on the door. Some give money and hope that nothing else is required. Some are overcome with compassion and identification. Some get taken for a ride. Some give until it hurts.

Joe turned up at our church office a while ago. I (Martin) was busy – very busy. He looked rough. He said he was on his way back home to Liverpool after visiting his daughter in south Wales. Apparently he'd used all his remaining money to get to our town and didn't have anything left to buy the ticket he needed to get back to Liverpool. Was he telling the truth? Did he 'deserve' help? Should I give him the money? This dilemma is a microcosm of the many situations in which we are confronted by the human face of poverty. Responding with love, grace and wisdom is not an exact science. I had to think on my feet. A few moments of reflection and I looked Joe in the eye and offered to take him to the station. I bought him a ticket and told him why I was helping him. He embraced me and departed. Was his story true? Was he hoping for cash to spend on drink rather than a rail ticket? I will never know.

The first thing we have to get sorted out in our minds is the big question we've been looking at – do people deserve to be helped? The argument of this book is that such language is judgmental and unhelpful. No one really earns the right to receive compassion, mercy and practical help. Once we start categorising the poor as deserving or undeserving, we are going to have to rethink whether we should bother to seek to rehabilitate criminals! After all, convicted criminals have done more than most to earn the designation undeserving and yet society is dedicating significant resources to their rehabilitation and reformation.

Now that we have seen that, from a biblical perspective, the notion of an undeserving poor is a myth, we can begin to take a much more practical and personal look at what we can do to address poverty on our doorsteps here in Britain.

SIMPLICITY – A PROPHETIC LIFESTYLE CHOICE

Western life is too cluttered. Everything we need is a click away and everyone seems to want to tell us about needs we didn't know we had! We all know we live in a materialistic culture – but what's the best way of engaging as Christians with this type of culture?

I (Martin) had an eye-opening experience one day. My wife and I had been talking to our friendly financial advisor. We'd discussed our financial situation and then he suddenly turned the conversation around to insurance. He told us about insurances we'd never heard of. It seemed as though we can insure more or less anything these days. Anyway, I found myself rather uncertainly signing up to a new insurance policy before he'd left our house. It seemed a good idea at the time, but the next day I had second thoughts. Do we really need income protection insurance? Where does faith come in? Where do you draw the line? What about using this money to give to the poor? I phoned up and cancelled the policy. You have to draw the line somewhere. The question for us all is this: where do you draw the line between your own needs and the needs of the world around you? No one can tell you the precise answer to that question – nor should they try! However, the worrying thing is that so few Christians are even asking the question.

Why not take an audit of your finances and your lifestyle? Where's the waste? What don't you need? Where can you simplify things a little? There are no absolute rights and wrongs in this process. It's very personal – but also very important. We must be careful not to be caught in the trap of our consumerist culture, where we keep living according to or even beyond our means, even when we have more than we need. All the time there are those around us struggling for basic necessities, it's imperative that we take a sober assessment of our own spending.

Simplicity is a good principle – and it is a useful summary of some of Jesus' key teachings on this issue. Let's take Matthew 6 as an example. Here are a few highlights: we are to avoid the danger of the alluring spiritual power of money; we are to give regularly and discreetly to the poor; we are to focus on advancing the Kingdom of God while exercising faith in God's provision; we are to avoid the unnecessary accumulation of wealth: we are to remember the fragility and temporary nature of material possessions when compared to eternal treasures.

These are some of the ingredients of what I like to call 'simplicity'. Jesus was unambiguous in calling us to this kind of lifestyle: it is part of our prophetic journey as Christians to engage with the poor through the heart of simplicity.

GENEROSITY – SACRIFICIAL GIVING ON BEHALF OF THE POOR

Most Christians give to their local church and to mission work. That's vitally important. But how many

Christians give specifically and sacrificially directly to the poor through personal contact, charities or church projects?

In the previous chapter we looked at an attitude of generosity, but what does this mean in practice? There's no better way of prioritising the poor than writing them into your budget! Small change in a charity collection box is one thing – planned sacrificial giving is quite another. Such giving challenges our heart attitudes but also releases great blessing both to us and to the recipients. My (Martin's) wife is more generous than I am. She frequently points out a serious need she wants us to support. She's my social conscience. I manage the money – she manages my heart attitudes! Whoever is challenging you, the important thing is to let yourself be challenged.

A couple I know divide their giving into three categories: their church, various charities and a 'poor fund'. They are always on the lookout for potential recipients of the 'poor fund' and because they have reserved the money they have no hesitancy over whether they can afford to make gifts to those in great need. There's always something in the fund.

Earlier we looked at the parable of the Good Samaritan (Luke 10:25-37) and it is particularly significant here. The story is well-known. It tells of an outstanding act of kindness enacted to a total stranger from a foreign culture. The Samaritan paid a price for his kindness: it cost him money and time, was inconvenient, and would possibly lead to social stigma. Jesus made several different points in telling this story. For our purpose, it's worth noting one in particular here that we saw in the previous chapter on attitudes: generous acts usually arise out of a generous heart, which is already predisposed to be aware of need and open to doing something about it. It's hard to imagine that the Samaritan would have stopped on the open road and intervened in such a major way to help the stricken man unless there was a prior openness. Such openness flows from the heart of generosity that is central to Christian discipleship.

Giving to the poor can be merely a token gesture. Sustained generosity requires openness, compassion, tough decisions and boldness. But like the apostle Paul, let's commit ourselves to being always mindful of those in need and 'remembering the poor'.

PROXIMITY – GETTING CLOSE ENOUGH TO NOTICE AND TO FEEL THE PAIN

My (Martin's) friendship with Brian changed my life. I met him while I was at university – he was begging in the city centre. Brian was in his fifties, no family, lonely, shabbily dressed, a heavy smoker and recently housed by the council after a period of homelessness. I kept meeting him in the same place in the city. We got talking and slowly built up an acquaintance. It took him a long time to open up and share. Then he invited me to his place – that was a big decision for him: no one else had been invited there. His basement room was always full of smoke, unventilated and dirty, but to Brian it was all he had and it was home. I went there to drink tea with Brian regularly for two years until I left university and left the city. My last meeting with Brian was painful and moving. He was clearly distressed – but so was I! Brian had become a friend. He was also a constant reminder to me that to be poor is to be very vulnerable in a society controlled by people with power.

There have been many other people in my life like Brian. People I have known and related to who constantly remind me that poverty is about people before it's about politics or charities or projects.

Sometimes Christians in countries such as Britain have a proximity problem when it comes to poverty. We need to be close enough relationally or physically to be in touch with the reality of poverty on a regular basis. Without proximity we are prone to prejudice. Jesus made this point too: "You will always have the poor with you, you can help them anytime you want" (Mark 14:7). Jesus expected his followers to be in proximity with the poor on an ongoing basis. Proximity leads to listening. Listening leads to empathy. There is no place for insulated middle class Christian communities seeing the poor only from a safe distance.

COMMUNITY – WORKING THROUGH THE LOCAL CHURCH, CHARITIES AND PROJECTS

Bill Hybels, the well known American church leader, has famously said that "the local church is the hope of the world". This provocative statement is true in many ways – not least in the context of tackling poverty. Churches as communities have remarkable capacity to get things done if they put their minds to it. They have in abundance what sociologists call 'social capital'. What they mean is that churches generally have high interest in social wellbeing, huge capacity to work in teams and great willingness to give time and energy generously.

For most Christians, by far the best way to invest in addressing poverty is through their local churches and through other local projects linked to churches. Poverty is not your personal responsibility alone – but you are (hopefully) part of a church through which much can be done. Working together, shared values, corporate prayer, leadership input, pastoral support – all these factors make churches the very best places in which to give our creative energies to help the poor.

There is no better example of this dynamic process at work in the New Testament than the church in Jerusalem at the very beginning of the story described in Acts. If you read the early chapters of Acts again, you'll notice a powerful combination of spiritual dynamism, strong relationships, good leadership, sharing of faith... and huge generosity to the poor.

I'm (Martin) sitting in a library as I write this chapter. As I leave the building I will walk past a small high street property that has been turned into a day centre for the homeless in our town. I enjoy visiting and chatting to the staff, and to whoever is sitting in their reception area drinking coffee. It's a project started by church people and now supported widely across the local community. Members of my church have served there over the years. Hundreds of similar community projects are to be found in every part of the country. Local opportunities to get engaged with poverty provide endless possibilities for the willing. Some readers may feel that they have no time in their busy lives to venture outside the parameters of their particular social group, working life or comfortable home location. Is that really true? We tend to make time for things that are really important to us.

STRATEGY – THINKING BEYOND THE IMMEDIATE NEED

Emergency relief is vital. Just as Accident & Emergency departments in local hospitals save lives, so do food-banks, soup kitchens, teams of Street Pastors, night shelters and many others. However, the world of church-based social action is much bigger than this. There comes a time in every Christian's life when we think about poverty issues and think that there must be more to helping the poor than crisis intervention. Some are called to be workers in the immediate task of helping the poor, but for others there are wider horizons to consider. There's the world of social enterprise. There's engagement in public policy. There's seeking office in local or national politics. There's working with statutory authorities. There are big campaigns needed from time to time. There are local partnerships to build in order to address specific issues.

On a visit to a church in Oxford some time ago I (Martin) was talking to a friend who told me a remarkable story. Through a prostitute who had become a Christian after 15 years of high-end brothel work, local Salvation Army church leaders became aware that human trafficking was an issue in their city. At the same time, God had been placing the issue of trafficking onto the heart of a lady named Sian, who was already setting up Christian social action projects for a large city-centre church. When Sian and the Salvation Army leaders spoke about trafficking in Oxford, they realised it was time to act, and so OXCAT was born.[49] The OXCAT team offered training to local police about human trafficking in the area, and in response the police adopted a more proactive approach and began to search out possible trafficking cases. This resulted in Oxford's first trafficking prosecutions (Papas and Cochrane in 2011[50]), followed by the much published Operation Bullfinch, which led to a child trafficking ring being smashed and seven men being sentenced to a total of at least 95 years in prison between them.[51] OXCAT continues to work right across Oxfordshire and beyond: raising awareness; supporting victims; and partnering with the police and other agencies in the battle to overcome trafficking.

The fact is that there's often a more strategic role for the local church than merely responding to immediate need. Some local research goes a long way. Prophetic leading is often the key. Sometimes something happens that just opens up the door to a strategic initiative. Such initiatives often lead the way towards addressing the underlying reasons for poverty and making a major impact on it.

So let's seek to be strategic – let's try to work out the big picture, not just respond to the immediate presenting need.

EXPECTANCY – FAITH FOR THE MIRACULOUS

The actions we have suggested so far could be adopted in one form or another by those outside the Church – they are not necessarily exclusive to Christians. However, we do have something to offer that others do not. We are not relying on our human effort to transform people's lives, but on a God who is intimately acquainted with the needs of the poor and offers hope as well as practical help. Jesus' response to human need combined compassion, prayer, commitment, faith, available human resources – and the expectation of miraculous change. We've already noted the extraordinary power and extent of his miracles in his earthly ministry. Christians have access to the same power that raised Jesus from the dead (Ephesians 1:18-20), and we should fully expect that power to be at work in us as we minister to the most vulnerable people in our society.

We have the privilege of praying for the people we are seeking to help. Faith and miracles must play a part in our care for the poor and needy. The Church's work with the poor cannot be reduced to a social services model. God's Spirit is available to us to bring miraculous breakthrough that goes beyond any practical help we can give. Not only does God call us to demonstrate his mercy to the poor, but we also get the honour of explaining the extraordinary good news of Jesus Christ that can be embraced equally by rich and poor alike, and which has immediate impact on lives, however desperate they may be. Let's be increasingly expectant for God to move in saving and transforming power as we reach out to those in need around us.

This chapter is where the rubber hits the road! One of the key aims of this book is to encourage all readers by sharing a big vision of both what the Bible says about poverty and also what can practically be done. As we each address the key issues of simplicity, generosity, proximity, community, strategy and expectancy, we may be surprised at the changes that begin to happen in our lives!

CONCLUSION –
A CHRISTIAN
PERSPECTIVE

While we may not have returned to the levels of poverty experienced in Victorian Britain, poverty in Britain is increasing and the outlook is far from rosy.[52] The State is less and less willing and able to meet the rising needs. Church leaders have been invited back to the table and have stepped into the fray of hotly contested debates about the deserving or undeserving nature of the poor in our midst.

Social action and social justice are back at the centre of the Church's agenda. But the prevailing myth that some of the poor are undeserving has infiltrated the Church. Where we should be standing up for truth, mercy, justice and compassion, too often we are buying the lies that most of the poor want to take advantage of us and don't really deserve our help anyway. Instead of being shaped by God's heart as revealed in the Bible, we can be too easily duped into believing political and media narratives.

I (Natalie) recently met a man begging in the streets, holding up a sign saying: 'Why lie? I want beer!' There's no question that the dominant narratives of our day would label this man as undeserving of my help. But intrigued by his sign, I asked him about it and how he had ended up here. He told me a little of his story: 18 years ago he became addicted to crack cocaine; more recently he had used alcohol to help him kick his crack habit, substituting one substance for another in the hope that it would do him less harm. He told me about his 16-year-old son, whom he was hoping to visit later.

I was touched by his story and reminded that everyone has one that explains how they got to where they are now. For him, begging for money for beer was a step in the right direction. It was progress; it was an improvement to his life. While it may be true that he was begging for money because of his own bad choices, I was mindful that I was once begging for mercy because of mine.

Should I give him money, knowing he would spend it on beer? I wasn't sure, but I was conscious that I didn't have anything else to offer him at that point – I was far away from home with no idea of what local services he might access or churches he might visit. In those few minutes talking with him, I contemplated the fact that I knew with some certainty, due to his sign, that he would spend any money I gave him unwisely. But I was also mindful that I cannot think of a time when God has withheld blessings from me – or even financial provision, actually – due to my lack of wisdom in handling them. One thing I knew for certain: this man was not undeserving of my help. He was facing many types of poverty and looking for some human kindness to help him through his day. Of course, my hope for him then and now is that he will find his way to treatment programmes and find freedom and faith. But at the time when I met him, all I could offer him was a small bit of mercy in the form of some conversation and a little loose change. Whatever was the right thing to do, I knew that I couldn't simply walk away.

As Christians, we are uniquely placed to offer hope, so it is time for us to recapture the heart of God for people in need. Many of us have already engaged with church-based projects helping those facing poverty in our local communities. The proliferation across our country of Christian initiatives that strike at the heart of poverty is good and right. Jesus told his disciples to "let your light shine before men, that they may see your good deeds and praise your Father in heaven" (Matthew 5:16). Many Christians and churches are turning their hands to various 'good deeds' that are making tangible differences on the ground – whether that is by feeding thousands through Foodbanks, contributing to reductions in public place violent crime as Street Pastors, or helping the long-term unemployed back to work through Job Clubs.

Christians are undeniably making their mark on British communities once again, but we are in danger of harbouring unhelpful and unbiblical attitudes to the poor, sometimes without even realising it. Often it only takes a gentle prod to reveal where we have bought into culture and myths – observing how we respond when someone acts like they have a right to our help and doesn't say 'thank you' is usually all it takes for us to see that we're still judging those in need based on their behaviour. Other times it is a simple challenge, such as those presented in these pages, to make a change to our lifestyles – to live differently to the consumerist culture around us – that starts to make us feel distinctly uncomfortable.

It is at these times that we must not be afraid to ask ourselves some penetrating questions about our attitudes and actions. What do we really think about the poor? Do we think some are undeserving of our help? How do we square this with the completely unmerited mercy we have received in Christ? When Jesus told the parable of the Good Samaritan, he was specific about the route the man took – it was the road from Jerusalem to Jericho, a steep descent along 17 miles or so of road, some of which ran through rocky, desert territory and was notoriously dangerous for lone travellers. But nowhere in the story does Jesus apportion blame to the man, even though he probably should have known better than to take such a risky route on his own. Instead, Jesus is concerned with how we should respond to the person in need as we come across them.

Jesus doesn't leave us room for excuse. Religious separation, cultural differences, even if the person is our enemy, he calls his people to a radical lifestyle of mercy and compassion. All too often our primary concern can be whether someone deserves our help, or what they'll do with what we give them, or whether we know the best way to help someone. But the primary concern of Jesus was showing mercy to people who came to him in need. Helping the poor is our responsibility; how they respond is theirs. When we actively cultivate biblical attitudes of human dignity, mercy, kindness, compassion, justice, and generosity, our hearts have no place to label any person made in the image of God as undeserving. When we commit ourselves to lives of simplicity, generosity, proximity, community, strategy and expectancy, we become far more focused on how God wants us to respond than how he wants others to act.

Understanding more of the Father's heart for those in need, imitating Jesus as our ultimate example of how to behave, and allowing the Spirit to prompt us to think and act differently – Christians are called to these things and are privileged to be Christ's ambassadors on the earth. As we reflect him increasingly, we will begin to shatter the myth of the undeserving poor.

NOTES

1. The OECD report's findings were covered by a number of media outlets, but this particular quote appeared in *The Telegraph* here: http://www.telegraph.co.uk/finance/economics/8935943/Gap-between-rich-and-poor-growing-fastest-in-Britain.html

2. http://www.ipsos-mori.com/researchpublications/researcharchive/3424/The-EconomistIpsos-MORI-Issues-Index-July-2014.aspx

3. Published in April 2013, the *Public attitudes to poverty and welfare, 1983-2011* report can be found here: http://www.natcen.ac.uk/media/137637/poverty-and-welfare.pdf (the quote is from page 2 of the Executive Summary).

4. There are a number of poverty statistics available to draw upon and they can be fairly complex, meaning that depending which period is taken and which measures are used, it can be argued that poverty is decreasing or increasing. At the time of going to print, the findings of the largest study into poverty ever conducted in the UK had just been released. These findings showed that, looking at a 30-year period, poverty has increased from 14% to 33%. (See http://poverty.ac.uk/editorial/pse-team-calls-government-tackle-rising-deprivation and http://www.theguardian.com/society/2014/jun/19/poverty-hits-twice-as-many-british-households.)

   Looking at the Government's own figures from 2012/13, the number of individuals in *absolute* poverty has risen to its highest level since 2001/02, though the figure is lower than those from 1998/99, 1999/2000 and 2000/01 (see page 4 here: https://www.gov.uk/government/uploads/system/uploads/attachment_data/file/325416/households-below-average-income-1994-1995-2012-2013.pdf).While the Government's 2012/13 child poverty statistics did not show much movement in either direction, the trajectory over the last 50 years is of great concern: the National Children's Bureau, which was established in 1963, has found that child poverty has increased over the last five decades and that the gap between children from affluent backgrounds and those in poverty is no smaller now than it was in the 1960s (see http://www.ncb.org.uk/who-we-are/celebrating-50-years/greater-expectations).

In addition, other specific types of poverty are rising, such as single parent working poverty (http://gingerbread.org.uk/news/259/working-poverty-rise).

Furthermore, the Institute for Fiscal Studies predicts that absolute and relative child poverty and absolute and relative working-age adult poverty will have risen by 2020-21 from its current level (see http://www.ifs.org.uk/comms/comm121.pdf).

5   See pages 12-13 of the *Public attitudes to poverty and welfare, 1983-2011* report, which was published in April 2013: http://www.natcen.ac.uk/media/137637/poverty-and-welfare.pdf

6   See, for example: http://www.theguardian.com/politics/2013/dec/21/iain-duncan-smith-food-banks-charities and http://www.independent.co.uk/news/uk/politics/iain-duncan-smith-accuses-food-bank-charity-the-trussell-trust-of-scaremongering-9021150.html

7   http://www.dailymail.co.uk/news/article-2563497/David-Cameron-criticised-benefits-reforms-26-Church-England-bishops-say-national-crisis-causing-poverty-malnutrition.html

8   Brown, M. (2014) 'The Church of England and welfare today' in *The Future of Welfare*, ed. Nick Spencer, p54. Published by Theos.

9   http://www.theguardian.com/society/2010/apr/15/ten-of-the-best-political-documents

10 http://www.theguardian.com/century/1940-1949/Story/0,,127564,00.html

11 Marshall, T. H. (1965) *Social Policy*, published by Hutchinson.

12 http://bsa-30.natcen.ac.uk/read-the-report/spending-and-welfare/welfare-benefits.aspx

13 http://www.telegraph.co.uk/finance/economics/8935943/Gap-between-rich-and-poor-growing-fastest-in-Britain.html

14 http://www.ukpublicspending.co.uk/past_spending

15 https://www.gov.uk/government/publications/households-below-average-income-hbai-199495-to-201213 ; https://www.gov.uk/government/uploads/system/uploads/attachment_data/file/325416/households-below-average-income-1994-1995-2012-2013.pdf (p6)

16 https://www.gov.uk/government/uploads/system/uploads/attachment_data/file/325416/households-below-average-income-1994-1995-2012-2013.pdf (p4)

17 http://www.cpag.org.uk/content/two-thirds-children-poverty-living-working-families

18 British Social Attitudes 29, published in 2012, p10, available here: http://www.bsa-29.natcen.ac.uk/

19 Vernon, M. (2010) 'Faith, hopes, and policy', *The Guardian: Comment is free – Cif Belief*, 3 July [Online]. Available at: http://www.theguardian.com/commentisfree/belief/2010/jul/03/religion-policy-faith-society

20 CST is based on a number of principles such as human dignity, charity, distributism (fair sharing of wealth), solidarity (identifying with other humans in need), and subsidiarity (ie giving individuals and communities as much responsibility as possible, rather than allowing the

State to take on too much). See http://www.catholicsocial
teaching.org.uk/

21 See, for example: http://www.catholic.org/news/hf/faith/
story.php?id=55361
22 See, for example: http://www.bbc.co.uk/news/uk-england-
merseyside-26613525 and http://www.csan.org.uk/
resource/csan-conference-2013-the-catholic-response-
poverty-crisis-lord-david-alton/. See also "The UK
Government's Big Society Programme & Catholic Social
Teaching." John Loughlin et.al., Von Hugel Institute,
2013
23 See, for example, the joint open letter to the leaders of the
three main political parties: http://www.theguardian.
com/society/2014/apr/16/million-people-britain-food-
banks-religious-leaders-faith-groups
24 John Stott, *Issues Facing Christians Today*, Zondervan,
1984. Subsequently republished: 1990, 1999, 2006.
25 www.streetpastors.co.uk
26 www.capuk.org
27 www.communitymoneyadvice.com
28 www.trusselltrust.org
29 See www.cinnamonnetwork.co.uk for further details
30 For example, see Jubilee+ (www.jubilee-plus.org) and the
Cinnamon Network (www.cinnamonnetwork.co.uk).
31 http://www.jubilee-plus.org/Articles/337911/Jubilee_
Plus/About_Us/Research/RESULTS_OF_THE.aspx
32 www.jointpublicissues.org.uk/truthandliesaboutpoverty
33 www.newstatesman.com/blogs/the-staggers/2011/06/
rowan-williams-government
34 www.christiantoday.com/article/church.condemns.
scrounger.rhetoric.against.poor/33107.htm
35 Williams, N. (2013), *Seen and not heard? How the
British national press represents Christianity in the public
sphere* (pp43, 45 and 42 respectively). Copies available
from natalie.williams@jubilee-plus.org.

36 Taira, T., Poole, E. and Knott, K. (2012) 'Religion in the British media today', in Gower, O. and Mitchell, J. (eds.) *Religion and the News*. Farnham, Surrey: Ashgate, p41.

37 Moore, S. (2012) 'Instead of being disgusted by poverty, we are disgusted by poor people themselves', *The Guardian*. http://www.theguardian.com/commentis free/2012/feb/16/suzanne-moore-disgusted-by-poor

38 http://djsresearch.co.uk/PublicConsultationMarket ResearchInsightsAndFindings/article/Survey-Highlights-Loss-of-Neighbourly-Spirit-in-UK-00239

39 British Social Attitudes 31, published in 2014, p121, available here: http://www.bsa-31.natcen.ac.uk/

40 http://www.cuf.org.uk/sites/default/files/PDFs/Research/ Bias_to_the_poor_Jan2012.pdf

41 https://www.gov.uk/government/speeches/launch-of-the-governments-consultation-on-better-measures-of-child-poverty

42 Hall, S (2013) *21st Century Welfare*, p6 – this Ipsos-MORI report is available here: http://www.ipsos-mori. com/researchpublications/publications/1520/21st-Century-Welfare.aspx

43 A similar framework has been proposed by Ed Silvoso in his 2007 book *Transformation*, published by Regal Books.

44 http://www.centreforsocialjustice.org.uk/policy/pathways-to-poverty

45 Tom, Niomi and Drey featured in *Breadline Kids*, broadcast on Channel 4 on 9 June 2014.

46 http://www.ncb.org.uk/media/571180/ecfchildpoverty. pdf

47 http://www.cpag.org.uk/content/impact-poverty

48 http://www.telegraph.co.uk/finance/economics/8935943/ Gap-between-rich-and-poor-growing-fastest-in-Britain. html

49 http://oxcat.org.uk/

50 http://www.bbc.co.uk/news/uk-england-oxfordshire-14728701
51 http://www.cps.gov.uk/thames_chiltern/cps_thames_and_chiltern_news/operation_bullfinch_men_sentenced___oxford/
52 See, for example: http://www.ifs.org.uk/comms/comm121.pdf and http://www.savethechildren.org.uk/sites/default/files/images/A_Fair_Start_for_Every_Child.pdf

Lightning Source UK Ltd.
Milton Keynes UK
UKOW02f2207190815

257203UK00001B/15/P